YATENGA

OTHER BOOKS BY PETER B. HAMMOND

Cultural and Social Anthropology, An Introduction (forthcoming)

Cultural and Social Anthropology : Selected Readings (ed.)

Physical Anthropology and Archaeology : Selected Readings (ed.)

Technology in the

Culture of a

West African Kingdom

YATENGA

PETER B. HAMMOND

The Free Press, New York

Collier-Macmillan Limited, London

This book
is lovingly dedicated
to my wife

PREFACE

My first interest in African cultures developed out of fascination with the research of Melville J. Herskovits and Frances S. Herskovits among New World Negroes. Later, as their graduate student at Northwestern University, my interest in Africa because of its relevance to the culture history of Negro Americans was complemented by a growing appreciation for the excitement of the continent itself as a context for the study of man. I came to be particularly interested in the French African territories, and in problems related to the achievement of technological and economic change. For this reason I went to France to study for a year at the Centre d'Initiation aux Problèmes Africains of the Institut des Hautes Études Politiques, the Sorbonne. At the end of that year, with the help of a travel grant from the High Commissioner for French West Africa, I made my first visit to the Mossi. At the conclusion of my pre-doctoral studies, I returned to Africa for eighteen months.

I went back to study the adjustment of Mossi workers to the technological innovations and economic changes imposed upon them at the Niger Irrigation Project in Mali, where several thousand Mossi have been resettled. I was interested in learning how the other aspects of traditional culture, particularly their social organization, political system, and religion had been affected by the technological and economic changes to which they were required to adjust. To understand this it was first necessary to become familiar with the culture of the Mossi in their homeland. Consequently, my first year in the field, from October 1954 to November 1955, was spent in the Kingdom of Yatenga, Upper Volta.

Most of the time I lived in the large village of Gourcy, traveling from there to other parts of Yatenga. The materials collected during this first phase of my field work are described here. My research among the Mossi settlers at the Niger Project has been reported elsewhere.

My work among the Mossi was handicapped by difficulties in the study of technology, especially the technologies of large societies, that still remain unresolved. The remarkable inattention which has so far been given to technology as a part of culture is reflected in the almost total lack of a developed method for its study. Ironically, those anthropologists who have argued most cogently for the significance of technology as an aspect of culture have failed so far to provide the techniques necessary to accurately test their important hypotheses.

At any rate, the problem resulting from the lack of such a developed method for study is serious. Two factors are critical to its resolution. One concerns present inadequacies in the training of anthropologists. The other relates to the conditions of field work as it is usually conducted. First, anthropologists, myself included, have not been and are not trained to either ascertain or assess the possible relevance of such factors as specifics of soil chemistry and climatic variations as they may affect technology. Equally important considerations such as the growth characteristics of plants and animals; or plant, animal and human diseases are usually even further beyond their professional competence.

Second, given the conditions under which most anthropologists work in the field—often alone and for a period of little more than a year—the sampling necessary for the adequate study of subsistence techniques and their product is often very difficult. The anthropologist studying farming, for example, can be on only one farm at a time, and can do little more than hope that the activities he observes are representative. The extent to which he can control for either environmental or technological variations is slight. If he is studying, as I was, a population of several hundred thousand his chances are poor of getting a representative sample of any aspect of the technology during the few short days when such critical activities as field preparation, planting, and the harvest are underway. And at such busy times he is unlikely to be successful in training or motivating local informants to help him in his necessarily frantic efforts.

To the problems of time and the extensiveness of territory and its variations there is added the equally serious problem of measures. For it is still far easier to study the techniques used in cultivation or the harvest than it is to measure their result, particularly on the scale necessary to yield data adequate for quantitative analysis. Even such a fairly simple task as surveying a field can be complicated by the resistance of the proprietor and his kinsmen for economic, religious, or political reasons, such as fear of taxation, punishment by the ancestral spirits, or causing annoyance to the village chief. And when such obstacles are overcome, only one field has been measured; one among thousands. To record the quantity of the farmer's harvest is likely to be an even harder task.

The measurement of less tangible but perhaps even more important factors such as labor productivity creates still greater difficulties. Work organization in African societies is always diffuse. In a single day a farmer may engage in a dozen distinct productive activities: cultivation of several crops in different fields; tool and house repair; hunting, gathering, extraction, and transport. While it is possible to obtain *examples* of such diffuse and varying work organization to acquire an adequate *sample* is nearly impossible.

Neither in my field work among the Mossi, nor in this account do I pretend wholly to have overcome any of these obstacles to the anthropological study of technology. I have attempted no more than the identification of technology as an aspect of African culture which merits scholarly attention. And I will be content if I am successful in stimulating the development of the rigorous techniques which such scholarly attention requires.

My stay among the Mossi was made possible by a Fellowship from the Foreign Area Research and Training Program of the Ford Foundation. It was facilitated by the cooperation of the French Government, and representatives of the Government of French West Africa at Dakar, Ouagadougou, and Ouahigouya. The staff of the Institut Français d'Afrique Noire at Ouagadougou, particularly Messieurs Le Moal and Savonnet, were also helpful. And I am indebted to the hospitality and cooperation of M. Dominique Zahan, then of the Office du Niger, for his hospitality and guidance as I began my field work among the Mossi. I must also acknowledge the assistance in the preparation of this book of the Anthropology Department, the Graduate School, and the Program of African Studies at Indiana University. My editor and friend, Mr. John D. Moore, read the entire manuscript and made many useful criticisms. Mrs. Madelyn Frohn typed the manuscript with patience and care.

A large measure of my thanks for help with this book must go to the Mossi of Yatenga themselves—especially to three good helpers and excellent friends who would want to be known here by their new Moslem names, Messieurs Salaam, Boukare, and Mamadou Ouedraogo.

CONTENTS

YATENGA

CHAPTER ONE

INTRODUCTION

There are two generally neglected, but basic and relevant dimensions
to attaining an efficient understanding of any culture. First the
manner in which the technology is integrated with the natural
environment must be comprehended. This integration must be
assessed in terms of its historical and contemporary relations to
the development of the other core aspects of culture: the economic
system, the social organization, the political system, and religion.[1]

   1.   Language and possibly esthetics might be added to this list. But
the study of language and the assessment of its relation to the other
aspects of culture is the work of specialists. Because I am not a linguist,
and inasmuch as several pioneering studies of the language of the
Mossi have been undertaken by scholars whose abilities surpass my
own, I have made no attempt to include language within the aspects
of culture considered here. As for esthetics, it does not qualify as a
core aspect of culture according to my criteria. Therefore it is
excluded. Not because Mossi art is not important, but because its
importance is not relevant to my analysis.

And second the manner in which this integration and its consequences have been affected by historical factors must be taken into
account. Essentially this is the approach that has been taken here
in the study of the Mossi of Yatenga.

In an important sense nearly every basic feature of the Mossi's
way of life is related to—and, to a degree, determined by—the
integration between their environment and their technology. The
origins of this integration and many of its specific attributes are,
of course, a consequence of the particular history of the Mossi.
And this historical variable will be referred to often. However,
Mossi history will be given less attention here in order to concen-
trate at greater length on a descriptive exposition of the core aspects
of their contemporary culture as these are affected by and affect
the integration between their environment and the technological
adjustment they have achieved to it.

The account given here will begin with a descriptive analysis of
this relationship. This will be followed by a description of the
other principal institutions of their culture: economy, social
organization, political system, and religion. In each instance an
attempt will be made to suggest, and to corroborate, the existence
of causal linkages between environment and technology and these
other aspects of Mossi culture.

This emphasis has been selected not in support of any particular
deterministic dogma, but because such a perspective allows for the
exploration of some problems of interest—ones that have been too
often neglected.

Such a focus on technology should be placed within the wider
context of African anthropology as it has developed so far. In the
past—until now, in fact—anthropologists working in Africa have
been principally concerned with only two of the many important
dimensions of the indigenous cultures of the continent: social
organization and religion. There are several reasons for this. The
first Europeans to come into contact with the peoples of Africa
were either colonial administrators or missionaries. The aspects of
African culture they set out to study were quite naturally those
most relevant to their own professional concerns. Colonial administrators were responsible for the successful perpetuation of political
domination over the indigenous peoples, for the regulation of conflict among them, and for such things as the collection of taxes. To

administer effectively they needed to learn something about the traditional organization of their subjects' societies. And they learned quickly that the kinship system, nearly everywhere in Africa, was most important both for ordering the life of the individual and for providing the structure basic to community life.

From the time of this early discovery there followed over the years an increasingly distinguished, subtle, theoretically elegant, and perceptive body of literature concerning the social organization, particularly the kinship systems, of Africa's peoples. Some of the earliest ethnographic work was done by colonial administrators themselves, men whose administrative responsibilities and long years of relative isolation among the people under their charge often resulted in the achievement of remarkably sophisticated insights into the structure and function of African social systems.[2] Later these early nonprofessional, but by no means amateur, scholars were replaced by trained anthropologists, usually social anthropologists in the African territories under British control and sociologists, or *ethnologues,* in the French areas. The same pattern was characteristic of the development of the early stages of anthropological inquiry in the former Belgian Congo. And in the parts of Africa under Portuguese control similar lines of scholarly investigation were followed, albeit somewhat erratically. For in these last areas the "underdeveloped" status of anthropological study was, and is, reflective of the general tendency toward stagnation that has been the consequence of the Portuguese presence in most parts of Africa. A similar but perhaps slightly stronger statement might be made about the Spanish African territories.

It was in Britain that scholarly attention to African social organization became most highly developed. And it is Britain that has made, at least until the last decade, the most outstanding contribution to the scientific understanding of African cultures. The methodological and theoretical formulations that have resulted from nearly fifty years of perceptive, disciplined British or British-sponsored field work in Africa have had a profound impact also on the development of anthropology as a science.[3]

2. See, for example, Robert S. Rattray, *Ashanti,* London: Oxford University Press, 1923, 2nd impression, 1955 ; and Maurice Delafosse, *Haut-Senegal-Niger,* 3 vol., Paris: Larose, 1911.

3. A necessarily brief list of examples of this would have to include

The first Europeans on the African scene who were not colonial administrators were most often missionaries. And again their interests in African culture were frequently reflective of their special professional concerns: religious conversion and the salvation of souls. They shared the administrators' interest in kinship organization because they sought to change it, to bring family life among their converts, especially in its sexual aspects, into closer alignment with the pattern of monogamy and middle-class morality characteristic of the missionaries' own cultural traditions.

And, of course, the missionaries were much concerned with religion. But the premise of the intrinsic inferiority of traditional African religion was basic to the justification of their presence. Consequently their studies of African religion contrast somewhat with the relative objectivity with which they were able to report on the social organization or other aspects of the cultures of the peoples with whom they came in contact.[4] On the subject of religion their Christian predilections proved to be a more serious obstacle to objectivity. The worth of their early descriptive accounts was accordingly diminished.

Like the colonial administrators, missionaries were followed by

such distinguished collections as Elizabeth E. Colson and Max Gluckman (eds.), *Seven Tribes of British Africa*, London: Oxford University Press on behalf of the Rhodes Livingstone Institute, 1951 ; A. R. Radcliffe-Brown and Daryll Forde (eds.), *African Systems of Kinship and Marriage*, London: Oxford University Press for the International African Institute, 1950 ; Meyer Fortes and E. E. Evans-Pritchard (eds.), *African Political Systems*, London: Oxford University Press for the International African Institute, 1940, as well as such classic ethnographies as E. E. Evans-Pritchard, *The Nuer*, Oxford: Clarendon Press, 1940 ; Meyer Fortes, *The Dynamics of Clanship among the Tallensi*, London: Oxford University Press for the International African Institute, 1945 ; most of the work in the Ethnographic survey of Africa sponsored by the International African Institute ; V. W. Turner, *Schism and Continuity in an African Society*, Manchester: Manchester University Press for the Rhodes Livingstone Institute, 1957 ; and Monica Wilson, *Good Company: A Study of Nyakyusa Age Villages*, London: Oxford University Press, 1951, to name only a few.

4.   See for example J. H. Oldham and B. D. Gibson, *The Remaking of Man in Africa*, London, 1931.

professional anthropologists who continued to study with greater
objectivity and superior results a subject that unfortunately, and
inexactly, they continued to call "primitive religion."[5]

Now there is no question but that the subject of social organization, and especially kinship, is absolutely basic to the achievement
of an efficient understanding of almost any other aspect of African
culture. Indeed it will be an important part of the argument presented here that this is so, that among the Mossi, as in every
indigenous African society without exception, the role of kinship
is primal in determining the formation of nearly all other social
groupings, and in sharply limiting and modifying their structure
and function.

The significance of religion as a core aspect of all African cultures
is equally clear. Most cause-and-effect relationships are explained
by Africans in religious and magical terms. And most traditional
activities are pervaded by an aura of supernatural sanctity. Religion
can seldom be ignored in studying any institution within any
African culture.

More recently Africanists have moved on to deal increasingly
with other aspects of African culture. Again, their interests have
sometimes manifested their practical concerns. There has, for
example, been a growing interest over the last decades in African
political and legal systems. The result so far has been a growing
body of equally erudite literature.[6] And finally the subject of African

5. Among the best of these: E. E. Evans-Pritchard, *Nuer Religion,*
London: Oxford University Press (Clarendon Press), 1956; S. F.
Nadel, *Nupe Religion,* London: Routledge and Kegan Paul, 1954;
Godfrey Lienhardt, *Divinity and Experience, The Religion of the
Dinka,* London: Oxford University Press, Clarendon Press, 1961;
and John Middleton, *Lugbara Religion,* London and New York:
Oxford University Press for the International African Institute, 1960;
as well as Daryll Forde (ed.), *African Worlds: Studies in the Cosmo-
logical Ideas and Social Values of African Peoples,* London: Oxford
University Press, 1954.
6. Among the best known and most important collections on
African political systems are those edited by Meyer Fortes and E. E.
Evans-Pritchard, *African Political Systems,* London: Oxford University
Press for the International African Institute, 1940; and by John
Middleton and David Tait, *Tribes Without Rulers,* London: Routledge
and Kegan Paul, 1958.

economic systems has lately been given more attention than it received in the past.[7]

There remains one aspect of African culture anthropologists have continued to ignore or, more precisely, to circumvent. Technology: the tools and techniques men use to modify conditions in their environment to meet their material needs.

The consistency with which technology is omitted is startling. For most of Africa's people live quite close to the level of subsistence— under harsh natural conditions they are able to modify only slightly. As a consequence, their means of getting a living—hunting, gathering, farming, and herding—are all relatively unproductive. Most Africans must spend most of their time working just to get enough to eat and to provide for their other basic material needs. Their technology occupies a preponderant part of their time, energy, intellect, and emotions. This absorption with subsistence tasks, and the nature of these tasks, is everywhere importantly related to the manner in which the African's other life activities are organized and carried on. Yet technology is ignored, even in otherwise exhaustive ethnographies.

Where technology is included, this is usually accomplished in a paragraph or two at the outset, unaccompanied by any effort to integrate it with the materials that follow. It is left up to the reader to relate such scanty data as he is provided to the analysis of proscriptive patrilateral cross-cousin marriage, witchcraft, or world view which follows. Where technology is considered at greater length, it is most often treated as if it were synonymous with economics, or both subjects are inappropriately subsumed under the limited rubric of material culture. There may be a brief description of house types, weaponry, and basket-making techniques, and that is often it. Sometimes such quick coverage is supplemented by the inclusion of a few geological, meteorological, botanical, and zoological indications—a worthy practice, in principle, but frequently useless in the absence of any suggestions as to the significance of such data.

7.   William Watson's study, *Tribal Cohesion in a Money Economy,* Manchester: Manchester University Press, 1959, is one of the best; and among the rare collections so far produced, Paul Bohannan and George Dalton (eds.), *Markets In Africa,* Evanston, Ill.: Northwestern University Press, 1962, is outstanding.

This general failure to consider the role of technology as a significant aspect of African culture relates to certain events in the early
history of anthropological theory and method as they developed in
Europe and the United States during the last hundred years. The
present blind spot most anthropologists have with regard to technology was not always there. The first travelers to reach native
peoples, not only in Africa, but also in the Pacific area and in the
Americas, reported extensively on the technologies of the indigenous
groups they encountered, and tools, containers, weapons, clothing,
and examples of shelter and vehicles used for transport were often
among the first artifacts sent off to European museums.

Upon receipt of these interesting objects there followed, often on
the part of scholars with no firsthand knowledge of non-European
peoples, an effort to correlate these artifacts with accounts of the
other aspects of the native peoples' cultures. And on the basis of
such correlations some theorists sought to establish an evolutionary
explanation of man's history—one in which particular levels of
technology were identified as determinants of particular levels, or
forms, of social, political, and religious organization.[8]

Such efforts were often unsuccessful, perhaps because of the too
great enthusiasm of some of these early scholars to seek oversimple
analogies between the dynamics of biological evolution and
historical process. Equally important causes of failure were their
lack of direct ethnographic field experience and the inadequacy of
the literature on the peoples whose cultures they tried to plot in
evolutionary perspective. The ease with which details of their
sequential schemata could be proven inaccurate frequently led to
rejection not only of their data, but also of the questions they were
asking and trying to answer.[9] Their antagonists, particularly
anthropologists in Britain and America, too often threw out the
theoretical baby with the empirical bath—and then returned

8. Many nineteenth-century scholars subscribed to this line of
thought. Important among them were Gustav Klemm, *Allgemeine
Cultur-Geshicte Der Menscheit,* Leipzig, 1843; A. Lane-Fox Pitt-
Rivers, *The Evolution of Culture And Other Essays,* Oxford: Oxford
University Press, 1916; John Lubbock (Baron Avebury), *Prehistoric
Times,* New York: Appleton, 1872.

9. This argument has been a long one and still goes on. For a good
brief synthesis of the anti-evolutionist view see M. J. Herskovits, *Man
and His Works,* New York: Knopf, 1950, p. 461.

righteously to their respective concerns with social structure and
culture history.

This overly spirited reaction against the work of early scholars
concerned with understanding the interrelationships between technology and the other aspects of culture received further stimulus
when aspects of the work of the cultural evolutionist Morgan were
taken up by Engels to provide cross-cultural validation for the
concept of dialectical materialism he was then developing.[10]

By a peculiar process of association, concern with technology
came to be equated with "materialism," and concern with materialism appeared to the uncritical to be dangerously close to Marxism.
And being a Marxist was irrefutably both inconvenient and bad.
The study of couvade and concepts of the soul were scientifically
just as rewarding, and far safer, lines of investigation. The subject
of technology was dropped. Or when it was studied, it was studied
alone. Suggestions concerning the interrelationship between technology and the other institutions of culture were to be abjured. The
tradition of avoidance thus established has been tenacious.

There have, of course, been some exceptions to this general
tendency. One is to be found in the work of White, some of his
students, and others whose work has taken a similar direction, perhaps as a result of his influence.[11] Steward and his students represent
another exception.[12] But neither of these scholars, nor those they
trained, have worked in Africa. And with one exception, the
possibly important implications of their work for African anthropology have not, so far, been considered.[13]

Quite recently, this trend has begun to be reversed. Murdock has

10.   Freidrich Engels, *The Origin of the Family, Private Property,
and the State,* London: Lawrence and Wishart, 1941.

11.   Leslie A. White, *The Science of Culture,* New York: Grove
Press, 1949 ; and *The Evolution of Culture,* New York: McGraw-Hill,
1959. Marshall D. Sahlins and Elman R. Service (eds.), *Evolution and
Culture,* Ann Arbor: University of Michigan Press, 1960.

12.   The most cogent aspects of Steward's argument are to be found
in *Theory of Cultural Change,* Urbana: University of Illinois Press,
1955.

13.   Marshall Sahlins, "The Segmentary Lineage: An Organization
for Predatory Expansion," *American Anthropologist,* Vol. 63 (1961),
pp. 322–45 ; reprinted in Peter B. Hammond (ed.), *Cultural and Social
Anthropology,* New York: Macmillan, 1964, pp. 181–200.

given extensive attention to the role of technology in Africa as it relates to such important phenomena as the Bantu migrations and the evolution of African social structure.[14] Both the theoretical work of Goldshmidt and the results of the fieldwork conducted by him in association with Winans, Oliver, and others are also evidence of a reversal in this trend.[15] And the collection of African ethnographies recently edited by Gibbs must also be excepted.[16]

The generally persistent error of ignoring technology as an important aspect of African culture can be pointed up in two ways. First, by attempting to document an instance in which the study of technology may be important for a comprehension of the development, structure, and present and future function of some of the other aspects of an African culture. And second, by providing evidence for the contention that the theoretical position so far associated with the study of technology is in no way antithetical to the historical and structuralist orientations to which it has too often and too facilely been opposed.

Here an effort will be made to accomplish these two things by indicating some ways in which a beginning understanding of the integration between the environment and the technology of a particular African people, the Mossi of Yatenga, may be related to the achievement of a better understanding of the structural and functional interrelations between the other aspects of their culture as it is today, as it was, and as it seems likely to change in the future.

14. George P. Murdock, *Africa, It's Peoples and Their Culture History,* New York: McGraw-Hill, 1959.

15. Walter Goldschmidt, *Man's Way,* New York: Holt, 1959.

16. James L. Gibbs, Jr., *Peoples of Africa,* New York: Holt, Rinehart, and Winston, 1965.

CHAPTER TWO

YATENGA AND ITS PEOPLE

Yatenga is one of the four Mossi kingdoms that now comprise a part of the West African Voltaic Republic. The population of Yatenga numbers approximately 700,000.[1]

To distinguish themselves from the ethnically similar peoples of the neighboring indigenous Mossi states of Ouagadougou, Fada-N'Gourma and Tenkodogo, and from the Mossi inhabitants of Kaya and Koudougou, the people of Yatenga call themselves yadese, a term that refers to their descent as a separate political group from the reign of Naba Yadega.[2]

Both the documentary evidence and contemporary oral traditions

1. This figure represents a compromise between the estimates made by Zahan (1961, p. 5) and Izard-Heritier (1959, p. 8) both of which are based on the seriously inadequate census data available on the Mossi of Yatenga.

2. Yatenga is a contraction of the terms Yadega and *tenga* (which can mean earth, village, a region, and community). Yadese is the plural of Yadega.

11

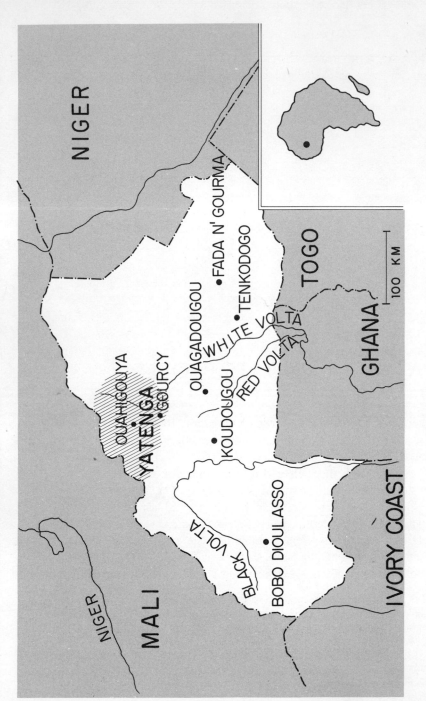

Republic of the Upper Volta

indicate that the events that led to the establishment of Yatenga
began, probably in the eleventh or twelfth century, with a struggle
for power at Ouagadougou.[3, 4] At the time Yadega's brother,
Kundege, inherited his deceased father's throne, Yadega was
residing at La, a village to the north. When he learned of his
father's death and returned to the capital to find his brother had
already assumed the kingship, he was resentful at losing his
chance to the succession and suspected that news of the death had
been deliberately withheld from him. In anger he quit Ouagadougou
and traveled north once more, this time to Gourcy where he
established the first capital of what was to become the Kingdom
of Yatenga. Soon afterward he was joined by his sister Pabre who
had stolen and brought with her the charms associated with kingship
at Ouagadougou. These charms are still at Gourcy, where they
are kept in a shrine built on the site of Naba Yadega's former
residence. In the eighteenth century, during the reign of Naba
Kango, a descendant of Naba Yadega, the capital of Yatenga was
moved still farther northward to its present location at Ouahigouya.

There were Mossi settlements in Yatenga before the establishment of Yadega's power there. These communities appear to have
been political dependencies of the Mossi kingdom of Tenkodogo.
Apparently the Mossi had begun to occupy the regions of Fada-
N'Gourma, Ouahigouya, and Tenkodogo as early as the eleventh
century, but it was not until the reign of Naba Yadega that their
political domination of the entire region was achieved.

   3.   Although the first monograph written on Yatenga (Noire, 1904)
places the reign of Yadega in the sixteenth century, other writers
prefer an earlier date. Vadier (1909, p. 2) estimates that the establishment of the kingdom occured in the twelfth century. Among later
scholars, all of whom based much of their work on these two early
monographs, M. Delafosse (*Haut-Senegal-Niger,* 3 vol., Paris: Larose,
1911) dates it from the eleventh, but Marc (1909, p. 186) and Tauxier
(1917, p. 672) assign Yadega's reign to the thirteenth century. For a
more detailed, if undefinitive, discussion of the dilemmas involved in
constructing an accurate chronology for the Mossi see Zahan (1961).
   4.   A transcription of the Mossi's own account of the events that
preceded the establishment of the Yatenga dynasty are presented in
more detail in Tauxier (1917, pp. 60 ff) and extensively quoted in
Zahan (1961, pp. 8 ff).

All the Mossi of the Voltaic region recognize that their ancestors came originally from the south, probably from Mamprusi and Dagomba in the Northern Territories of what is now Ghana. In this regard Yatenga appears to be typical of many states of the Voltaic region whose populations represent the amalgamation of autochthonous and immigrant peoples. Acknowledging that "We owe to Rattray the discovery that these central Voltaic tribes are composed of two major groups of communities," Fortes has described this general pattern succinctly:

> On the one side are those that claim to be descendants of immigrants from parts of the country other than their present habitats. On the other side are communities that claim to be the autochthonous inhabitants. The two groups are found in every tribe, including the Mossi, Mamprusi, and Dagomba, living side by side and indistinguishable from one another by broad cultural or linguistic criteria. Many of the immigrant communities claim descent from forebears of the Mampuru ruling stock. Though now wholly amalgamated with the alleged aboriginal inhabitants, they have certain ritual observances and a system of chieftainship similar to those of the Mamprusi. . . . The institution distinctive of the autochthonous communities is the office of "Custodian of the Earth." This ritual office, involving priestly functions in connection with the cult of the Earth, is found among many West African peoples from the Senegal to the mouth of the Niger. In the Voltaic region it is the exclusive prerogative of the autochthonous communities.[5]

From an examination of the contemporary "ethnographic picture" Fortes infers that

> . . . the population of the Voltaic region was, in the past, constantly being redistributed by migrations of small groups. . . . The fact that such migrations have gone on in the recent past, and are still going on in the central area suggests that these migrations were

5.   Meyer Fortes *The Dynamics of Clanship Among the Tallensi,* London: Oxford University Press for the International African Institute, 1945, p. 6, 7. D. Zahan (1961, pp. 16 ff) believes the structural opposition between these groups has been over simplified and over stated and suggests any analysis of Mossi culture history and social structure must take into account their cosmogyny. He seems to contend that social reality among the Mossi is the result of a mystical concept, that theirs is a social order "geometriquement ordonné." For an evaluation of his interesting argument, which I am not personally competent to assess, see Pageard (1962).

"The Mossi are a handsome Negro people of a type characteristic of the Western Sudan . . ."

the result, rather of ecological pressures and social forces than of large-scale conquests.[6]

Both the tradition of southern origin mentioned previously and the lack of a history of extensive warfare between the Mossi and the indigenous inhabitants of Yatenga support this statement.

Two ethnically separate groups inhabited the region of Yatenga prior to the Mossi immigration. One appears to have remained and to have assimilated Mossi culture, the other evidently fled. The Mossi refer to this first group as Nyonyose. In the southwestern region of Yatenga some Nyonyose communities have retained their ethnic distinctiveness. Throughout most of the country, however, the people known to be their descendants usually are referred to as Mossi. Control over the supernatural forces of nature is the prerogative of these indigenous inhabitants of Yatenga. Only they can be Earth priests, the ritual guardians of man's relationship to his natural milieu; conversely they are denied the exercise of political power so that even those villages inhabited exclusively by Nyonyose are governed by Mossi chiefs. Apparently some Dogon also inhabited the region of Yatenga prior to the arrival of Naba Yadega. But with the consolidation of his power there, they moved northward to their present habitat, in the Bandiagara escarpement of eastern Mali.

Most Mossi communities are inhabited by another recently arrived group, the Yarse, who are probably of Mende origin.[7] The Yarse participate fully in Mossi culture and intermarry with them freely. However, like the other non-Mossi inhabitants of Yatenga, they are denied access to political power.

The Fulani herdsmen, who live throughout Yatenga for part of the year, tend the Mossi cattle in return for gifts of grain and grazing rights on their land. They carefully maintain their separate cultural traditions and marry only among themselves or with the Silmi-Mossi, a group said to have originated from what is now regarded as a prohibited union, between a Fulani and a Mossi, and

6.   Meyer Fortes, *The Dynamics of Clanship Among the Tallensi,* London: Oxford University Press for the International African Institute, 1945, p. 7.
7.   Tauxier (1917).

whose way of life manifests the fusion of their disparate cultural
origins.

The Mossi are a handsome Negro people of a kind characteristic
of the Western Sudan. They are tall, well muscled, slender, and
dark brown. Men and women are cicatrized vertically with lines
from the temple to the lower jaw and with diagonal cuts from the
bridge of the nose outward over the cheek. The women are also
scarified on the breasts and abdomen—as a mark of beauty and
character. The Mossi believe that a young woman who will endure
the discomfort of such efforts at embellishment in order to be pleas-
ing to men will also be more likely to undertake willingly her share
in the hard work necessary to please men in other ways—in the
house and on the farm. Mossi women wear their hair in rows of
small braids worked close to the head from front to back. Sometimes their upper teeth are filed to a point, another embellishment
indicative of character. Women with full flat faces are much
admired.

The traditional dress of the women—still worn by most of them—
consists of a skirt wrapped around the waist and reaching to mid-
calf, which is made from sewing together narrow bands of woven
cotton, often in alternating colors with blue, white, and red pre-
dominating. Now such skirts are sometimes made of trade cloth
in which the fashionable colors and patterns vary from year to year.
Women usually tie up their heads in cloths of a complementary
color and design. Their wrists and hands, and sometimes their
ankles, are decorated with rings and bracelets of copper and brass.
When not barefooted they wear thong sandals, now most often
made of brightly colored plastic strips.

Mossi men are heavily muscled, especially in the chest and arms,
with slender hips, small salient buttocks, and long legs that often
seem disproportionately thin below the knee. Most men shave their
heads, and beards frequently fringe their jaws from ear to ear. The
traditional dress of the men is also made from woven bands of
cotton. These are sewn together to make loose-fitting, knee-length
trousers, over which are worn sleeveless tunics of the same material.
Caps are made of cotton cloth or of woven strips of white, red-
brown, and black woolen bands pulled together at the tip with a
tassel.

Mŏré, the language of the Mossi, belongs to the Gur subfamily of the Niger-Congo family of languages.[8] In *Mŏré* the Mossi have a rich oral literature which they rely upon frequently as a means of embellishing their speech. Even casual discourse is full of parables and allegories, and on formal occasions a man's cultivation is indicated by the elegance of his imagery and his facility in drawing upon the extensive store of Mossi proverbs to illustrate his points.[9]

Mossi village communities are comprised of a number of dispersed neighborhoods, each of which contains the majority of the male members of a patrisib. In turn, these neighborhoods are formed of loose clusters of patriclan residences usually containing several patrilocal extended families. Such residences may contain from five to one hundred individual dwellings. The houses are round, made of mud, and topped with conical thatch roofs. Each has its own courtyard. The outer sides of the houses and courtyards join to form an external wall enclosing the entire residence. The neighborhoods, and even the compound residences themselves, are separated from one another by the bush, farmlands, and the public way, giving a single Mossi village the appearance of a loose cluster of small walled towns.

The Mossi are farmers. Their scattered compound dwellings and their granaries of thatch and mud are surrounded by the fields on which they grow the cereals, principally millet and sorghum, that are the basic items in their diet. During the dry months these fields are dusty and barren, and the progressive erosion to which they are subject is everywhere apparent. Only a few carefully watered kitchen gardens remain green during the long months, from October to May, when there is no rain. But once the rains begin, the stark landscape is transformed. Much of the stick-dry brush is quickly covered with tender leaves, wild grasses line the pathways, and as the rains fall more heavily the rapidly growing stands of millet and

8.   Joseph H. Greenberg, "The Languages of Africa," *International Journal of American Linguistics,* XXIX (January, 1963), p. 8.

9.   Several collections of these proverbs have been made for the Mossi of Ouagadougou, who speak a somewhat different dialect (cf. G. Alexandre, *Mös yel - buna,* Mission des Pères Blancs, 1954) ; however they are in the vernacular and no translation is provided. For the Mossi of Yatenga there is only the small list of proverbs contained in John F. Hall, *Dictionary and Practical Notes, Mossi-English Languages,* Mission des Assemblées de Dieu, Ouahigouya, Upper Volta, n.d.

"During the dry months the fields are dusty and barren . . ."

sorghum all but obscure the Mossi settlements. When the rains
end and the harvests are over, many young men leave to seek
work in the cities of the Sudanic region, in Ouagadougou, Bobo-
Dioulasso, Mopti, and Bamako; or they go south to the plantations
and to the towns and ports of Ghana and the Ivory Coast. The
Mossi who stay behind turn to the repair of their household goods,
their tools and weapons, and to such crafts as basketry and the
manufacture of cloth. Men hunt. Women and children give more
attention to the gathering of wild foods. And everyone participates
enthusiastically in the cycle of rituals of thanksgiving that close the
year just ended and open the season to come.

Despite a period of almost fifty years of French colonial control
the relation between the traditional technology of the Mossi and
the other institutions of their culture has remained relatively unchanged. Because the country is poor in known mineral resources,
in apparent agricultural potential, and in manufactures, there was
little reason for the French to disturb the indigenous technology
and economy of the Mossi. And they did not.

The continuity of indigenous Mossi culture is importantly related
to this fact. As a result of the absence of technological innovation
and economic change, traditional social relationships were left
largely intact. Even the political system lent itself sufficiently well
to the requirements of indirect rule to obviate the direct imposition
of colonial authority.

The persistence of the traditional patterning of the technology,
the economy, and the social and political systems explains the
apparent absence of need for religious change manifested in the
perpetuation of the traditional belief system of the Mossi and the
relative lack of success of both Moslem and Christian efforts at
proselytizing.

Forced labor recruitment and the seasonal migration of workers
to neighboring West African territories were the most significant
innovations resulting from European control of Yatenga. However
in providing an alternative, external means of making a living and
achieving some measure of economic and social mobility, they
reduce the pressure for change in the traditional organization of
Mossi society. But the alternative provided is only temporary. The
relation of the Mossi to such alien milieux rarely offers a
sufficiently secure alternative to discourage continued participation

"But once the rains begin the stark landscape is transformed . . . the rapidly growing stands of millet all but obscure the Mossi settlements."

in their traditional culture. Most Mossi finally return home. In these two ways labor migration has acted indirectly to reinforce the commitment of the Mossi to support the traditional patterns of their culture.

To achieve an understanding of the problem with which my field work was principally concerned, the relation of the traditional technology of the Mossi to the rest of their culture, my first year among them was spent observing the annual cycle of productive activities as it moved from the first rainmaking ceremonies, through the sacrifices that precede planting, to the organization of cultivation, the harvest, and the concluding festivals of thanksgiving.

The success of the Mossi farmer's endeavor during this yearly round depends on his relation to two integrated sets of forces: those that order his social environment and those that vitalize his natural milieu.

In his social environment the Mossi is most importantly affected by his relation to the living members of his patriclan, patrilineage, and patrisib and to his ancestral spirits. His lineage elders grant him the right to his land, which he would be unable to work without the help of his wife or wives and his lineage mates; and he is equally dependent on them for assistance if his crop should fail. To be assured of this essential cooperation, he must work to maintain his position within the intricate network of rights and obligations characteristic of the Mossi kinship system, a task that requires frequent exchange of visits and presents, economic and ceremonial assistance, and constant participation in clan and lineage affairs. The security of the Mossi's position within the village community and within the political system is achieved by means of an analogous sort of subordination.

The second principal set of forces on which the Mossi farmer is dependent are supernatural. He must maintain the goodwill of the ancestral spirits who have entrusted the land to him and his kinsmen, their living descendants. Whether they will give or take away the good health he must have to carry him through the arduous activity of the rainy season when work is hardest and food is in short supply depends on his attention to their ceremonial needs. If he feeds them a chicken, they may bring the "souls" from a neighboring stand of millet to enrich his own fields, and they can be relied on to protect his shea nut trees from the high winds that might otherwise destroy their yield. He forgets the ancestors at his peril.

The terrestrial, climatic, and vegetal manifestations of Wennam, the Mossi supreme deity, are also important to the farmer's well-being. These are propitiated through the Earth priests. By their intercession with the supernatural forces of nature, the farmer is assured of the benevolent natural conditions equally essential for the success of his agricultural endeavor.

The reliance of the people of Yatenga on these interdependent sources of social and supernatural well-being is dramatically acted out in the ritual observances that accompany each phase in the technological cycle of the Mossi year.

CHAPTER THREE

MOSSI TECHNOLOGY

To abstract Mossi technology from the matrix of economic, social, political, and religious institutions of which it is an integral part is to risk a distortion of reality. First, because the significance of technology as an aspect of Mossi culture, contributing basically to the structure, function, and perpetuation of their particular pattern of living, can only be accurately perceived and assessed as it operates in context. And second, because many of the actions the Mossi regard as essential parts of that system of techniques upon which they rely to make a living are, from the anthropologist's point of view, more properly to be considered as aspects of their economic organization, kinship system, or ideology. Such actions, for example, as the subordination of individual interests within the productive unit formed by the family, reliance on the authority of lineage elders in the performance of tasks, propitiation of the ancestral spirits who protect the farmers' health, and sacrifices to the earth deity which assures soil fertility are all regarded by the

25

Mossi as vitally related to the successful operation of their technology.

So long as the dangers of such distortion are borne in mind, technology, like the other aspects of Mossi culture, can be abstracted for analysis.

THE ENVIRONMENTAL CONTEXT

Mossi technology operates under a particular set of environmentally imposed conditions—harsh conditions that have affected the development of technology in several important ways. For given the simplicity of this technology—that is, the relative inefficiency of the means available to the Mossi for modifying natural conditions of soil, climate, and biotic milieu—they have had to develop and adapt their techniques for getting a living to such conditions much as they have found them.

Climatic conditions in Yatenga are fairly well suited, if not optimum, to the cultivation of the cereals, mostly millets and sorghum, that are the basic elements in the subsistence technology of the Mossi. The year is marked by two principal seasons, one wet, when there is often too much rain, and the other hot and dry when no rain falls at all. There are from twenty-five to slightly more than thirty inches of rainfall each year between the months of May and October. Although the duration and abundance of the rains vary from year to year, the wet season is usually well under way by June, the first light showers having begun in early May. At the height of the season, in July and August, the rains are often accompanied by violent nocturnal wind storms that carry off thatch roofs, tear the tops from storehouses, and whip dangerously the ripening stalks of grain. Sometimes fields are swamped, and excess moisture prevents the crop in other fields from maturing and setting before the harvest.

The White Volta, the only river in Yatenga, rises after the first rains. Many streams overflow their banks, and ponds and natural depressions fill up quickly. The clayey soils of the roads and paths swell to a gluey consistency. When it rains very hard, even the mud walls of the Mossi houses begin to melt.

The intensity of the rains increases steadily until mid-August. Frequent showers and occasional storms are interspersed with hot sunny intervals, lasting from hours to several days, when the sky is bright blue and filled with floating white clouds. In good years these periods of warm, clear weather increase in duration as the season nears its end. By early September such warm spells are essential to allow for the full maturation of the millet, and, once the harvest is begun, to permit the drying of the crop before it is carried off to the granaries for storage.

Beginning in late October the Mossi face many months of dry, hot weather. Heat and aridity increase as the season progresses. Early mornings in November are often chilly, but by late March the noonday sun frequently sustains temperatures well above 115°. Gradually the streams and ponds retreat to silty beds that are soon baked to the consistency of hard cracked clay. Some of the wells go dry. Others must be deepened. And late in the season the brown and brackish water the Mossi bring up in their skin buckets often tastes of earth.

From time to time the harmattan, a hot wind from the Sahara, blows down on Yatenga, picking up the dust to create a stifling atmosphere of ochre haze and dull red sunlight. But on most days during the dry season the skies are a hot cloudless white.

Lying between 13 and 14 degrees north of the equator, Yatenga occupies the upper reaches of that belt of orchard bush, savannah, and scrubland that stretches northward from the fringes of the Guinea forest to the southern borders of the Sahara. For the most part the terrain is almost surrealistically stark and flat. Elevation varies between two and three thousand feet above sea level, but there are no mountains, and the monotony of the plains is only infrequently interrupted by low hills and jagged piles of lateritic boulders.

The land is poor.[1] Almost everywhere a thin, gravelly red soil, rich in iron but poor in humus, lies just above a hard layer of ferruginous rock. The poverty of the soils in Yatenga is explained by a viciously circular process of debilitation that begins when the Mossi farmers allow their fields to be overgrazed in the dry season. Whatever meager brush remains is burned off before the first rains that precede planting. The manure and potash this provides are an inadequate substitute for the loss of vegetation that

1. For more on the poverty of the Mossi soils and the problem this creates see Izard-Heritier and Heritier (1958).

would otherwise serve to enrich the soil. Consequently each year
the new crop of millet takes nutrients from the earth that are only
partially replaced. Because decaying organic matter also holds
water in the soil, the lack of humus causes still more rapid evapora-
tion, erosion, and leaching. This, in turn, produces still hotter, drier
soils and poorer plant growth. Where deeper soils begin to form,
the Mossi carry them off to spread over sandy spots in other poorer
fields or to make gardens. Ultimately the fragile cover of dusty
topsoil is removed altogether to leave extensive areas of useless
lateritic pan that must be abandoned, thus increasing the pressure
to use to exhaustion the land that remains. By this slow but
insidious process first fields and finally whole farms must be given
up. And the Mossi cultivators are often forced to leave their villages
to search for new land. Expectably this process is most accelerated
and its dessicating consequences are already most marked in the
northern part of Yatenga, closest to the Sahara.

The progressive impoverishment of the soils and the dramatic
reversals characteristic of the climate are naturally reflected in the
vegetational cover. Most of the year the countryside is dun colored
and dry; the only greenery is provided by a few dusty tufts of brush,
the leaves of sparsely scattered trees, and an occasional meager
garden kept haphazardly alive with water arduously carried from
the well. But when the rains begin, the landscape is rapidly
modified by an aura of delicate, quickly deepening green. The
rising streams and ponds are lined with new growth. Lush wild
grasses and thick shrubs soon cover the rest of the barren ground,
and farmers must work incessantly to protect their young crops
from the rampant spread of weeds.

Little of this suddenly abundant vegetation is wasted. One way
or another, most of the annually appearing wild plants are consumed, eaten by the herds of the Fulani or by the Mossi's own
animals, or gathered by the women and children for food, fodder, or
firewood. Even the weeds chopped out during cultivation are left
to dry and are then gathered to feed the sheep and goats kept in
pens during the rainy season. Most of the remaining vegetation
quickly withers away as the temperature climbs and the rains end.
Whatever brush remains is later burned off, and soon the land is
brown and barren once more.

Useful fauna is as scarce in Yatenga as perennial vegetation.

Although Mossi folklore refers to lions and elephants, today a variety of small antelope and several species of rodents, as well as a few wild Guinea fowl and rabbits, are the only game available; some fish are found in the river, the streams, and in the larger lakes. Unfortunately insects are more abundant. Occasionally invasions of desert and migratory locusts swoop down to destroy the year's food supply of an entire community in a few hours. The anopheles mosquito and *Aedes aegypti,* the carrier of yellow fever, are both present in Yatenga, but luckily the arid conditions that prevail for much of the year serve to control their spread. The Guinea worm, often growing under the skin to a length of several feet and causing swelling, ulceration, debilitation, and severe pain, is a more persistent pest. Filaria worm is a widespread cause of blindness.

The Mossi cannot control the depredations of these insects nor of the many maladies—measles, smallpox, leprosy, yaws, trachoma, syphilis, and malnutrition—from which they suffer.[2] Their efforts to modify the effects of climate, the chemistry of their soils, and the quality of the plants they grow are equally ineffective. They must adjust to their harsh environment much as they find it, being able neither to modify its basic characteristics nor to anticipate or control its occasional sharp changes. Bearing these factors in mind, their technology can be appreciated for its ingeniousness even as it must be assessed as relatively unproductive.

FARMING

First of all the Mossi are farmers. Millet cultivation is their basic subsistence activity, the way they acquire most of the food that keeps them alive. The primacy of farming in the organization of their lives is manifested in nearly every aspect of their culture—in

2. I can only assert "intuitively" that the effects of chronic malnutrition on the behavior of the Mossi need to be better understood. It is expectable that prolonged dietary deficiency would affect mental development, the processes of cognition, and many aspects of behavior, not alone the performance of those tasks related to the subsistence technology. Unfortunately there has been only one detailed account of nutrition among the Mossi of Yatenga (Serre, 1953). And no effort is made in that report to evaluate the data it contains in terms of their possible relevance to the satisfaction of the basic nutritional needs of the Mossi or to the relation of Mossi nutrition to behavior.

the organization of work and the distribution of the products of work, in the organization of the family, society, and the political system, in their values, and in their religious ideas and practices.

The tools they use to farm are very simple. A mattock, a hoe, and a knife are their principal implements. The mattock has a double end, one part hoe and one part short hammer, and is used principally in cleaning and clearing the fields—for chopping out large roots and for breaking up the larger clods of dry earth. The hoe used in planting and cultivation is of a type found widely in West Africa. It is made by the Mossi smiths from a long thin metal blade hafted to a strong two-foot long stick. The blade is attached to a side branch; the main branch serves as the handle. A knife with an eighteen-inch cutting edge attached to a wooden handle wrapped in leather is used at harvest time to chop off the heads of grain and to cut down the millet stalks. Seeds for planting are carried in a gourd or in a leather pouch. A small basket is sometimes used at the harvest for collecting the millet panicles. These are the only farm tools the Mossi have.

"Ki" is the generic term for the cereals, principally millet and sorghum, that are the dominant staples in the Mossi diet; from 60 to 90 per cent of the land under cultivation is devoted to these crops. Several factors explain their importance. They require relatively little water, they do not demand rich soil, they can survive by remaining dormant during periods of drought, they are able to withstand intense dry heat, and their short growing period assures maturation during a rainy season too brief for many other plants.

Cattail millet [kasuya (Pennisetun spicatum and P. typhoideum)] is cultivated somewhat more extensively than sorghum, perhaps because it germinates most rapidly in the dry soil, progresses most quickly with the early light showers that mark the first phase of the rainy season, and is well established before the onset of the heavy rains of July and August. At maturity the plants reach a height of five or six feet. The millet grains, contained in a compact spike at the head of the plant, dry out and set during the increasingly long periods of warm clear weather which, in good years, occur in September and October just before the harvest.

Kenda, a red-seeded variety of sorghum (S. vulgare), also appears to be well adapted to growing conditions in Yatenga, and it too is

"First of all the Mossi are farmers . . ."

extensively cultivated. Its stalks reach an even greater height at maturity, between six and twelve feet. Sorghum grains are also produced in clusters at the top of the plant. Fonio [*kew (Digitaria exilis)*], an inferior millet, is the least extensively cultivated of the Mossi staple cereals. Very often it is sown in fields planted with cattail millet, which matures more slowly and thus does not interfere with the growing space of the fonio which attains a height of no more than two feet at harvest-time.

Maize *(kamana)* is widely cultivated. However, because it is more vulnerable to drought and high temperatures, requires more careful cultivation, and is especially exhausting to soils where fertilizers are lacking, it is usually grown as a secondary crop in fields close to the Mossi farmer's dwelling. Because it matures more rapidly than millet, it can be harvested early when food, especially grain stored from the previous year, is becoming scarce.

Several edible legumes are also cultivated as field crops. Peanuts [*soom kam (Arachis hypogea)*], Bambara ground nuts *(Voandzeia subterranea)*, and Bengal beans are usually grown in the thin dry soil they tolerate so long as it is sufficiently friable to allow penetration of their roots. As creepers these legumes provide good ground cover during the rainy season and are sometimes interplanted with millet. They mature earlier than the cereals. When the seeds are picked, the plants themselves are usually chopped under, one of the rare instances in which the Mossi use green manure. Sometimes the young leaves of the Bengal bean are picked and eaten as a vegetable.

Cotton is also cultivated as a field crop by the Mossi. Certain other minor crops are grown along the margins of the fields or in sectors where the soil is especially suited to their needs. The shrubs that bear sesame seeds and sorrel are grown in this manner, for example, and occasionally okra, eggplant, and a few rows of tobacco are sown as field crops or along the edges of a millet field.

Cereals are most often cultivated in the larger fields located some distance from the settlement. Those nearer the habitation, although sometimes planted to grain, are more frequently used for secondary crops. Fields free from stones and with a loamy topsoil are, of course, preferred for the cultivation of all crops, but the amount of such land is rarely adequate to the farmers' needs. In selecting new land or fallow fields for replanting, the Mossi farmer is guided by the natural vegetational cover as an indication of soil fertility. A field that is thickly covered with wild grasses during the rainy season is usually thought to be a good prospect. But land is almost always put back into cultivation before it is fully regenerated, a process that would take twenty to thirty years.

Fields close to the household settlement tend to be most constantly in use. The consequent tendency for them to be more quickly exhausted is to a certain extent checked by the greater ease with which they can be fertilized, usually with the collected droppings of goats, sheep, and burros. The more distant fields are often fertilized during the dry season by the herds of the Fulani or by the farmer's own flocks of sheep and goats. Although a certain balance is maintained so long as both types of field are in use, it is ultimately upset by the greater difficulty of fallowing near the homestead, because the wild plants that would serve to restore the soil are most accessible for grazing animals and for the collection of fodder, and because such lands are most readily available for conversion into gardens. And it is this land that is most carefully burned off during the dry season, thus exposing the soil to erosion and leaching when the rains begin. As a result the Mossi households are often surrounded by totally barren stretches of laterite, which are extended each season in gradually growing concentric circles of ruined earth.

As his field becomes increasingly impoverished, the Mossi farmer relies progressively on the practices of crop rotation, fallowing, and shifting cultivation. Land, either virgin or recovered from fallow, is planted to millet for the first three years. The fourth year it may again be set into millet, or, if the last crop has not been good, it is often seeded to cotton, which is believed to renew the soil because of the intensive cultivation it requires and the practice of chopping under the plants for green manure. However a field is rarely planted to millet for more than five consecutive seasons. After two intervening plantings of cotton it may again be seeded to millet for three years. Then it is usually put into peanuts, another year of cotton, then millet again for a season or two, and perhaps another planting of cotton. Finally, before it is left fallow, it may be planted with inferior millet.

Well-fertilized field crops are rotated less often and fallowing can be delayed for a longer period. The length of a fallow is generally not calculated in terms of years, but is determined both by the farmer's need for land and his judgment of the degree of regeneration a particular field has undergone. An exhausted field may be left fallow for five, ten, or fifteen years.

Analytically, shifting cultivation can be distinguished from fallowing when so much of a farmer's land is exhausted—as was stated, the process of soil regeneration often takes several decades—that sufficient arable land can only be found at an inconvenient distance from his original residence. Then the farmer's household is often shifted to be closer to his new fields.

Sometimes he moves off alone, accompanied only by the members of his elementary family. More often the Mossi move as extended or joint family groups. But such groups rarely include more than twenty persons. When they leave the compound residence of their patriclan to resettle closer to their farms, their abandoned fields usually return to bush, a process that serves both to restore the top soil gradually and to check the spread of crop diseases by destroying their hosts. Ultimately, of course, such land is reclaimed either by members of the former proprietors' kin group or by other farmers. Thus what from the standpoint of the individual farmer may appear to be shifting cultivation is, in terms of the Mossi local community, sometimes only a protracted system of long fallowing.

By this process whole communities may in some instances be gradually displaced. Because population increase among the Mossi has so far been unaccompanied by a significant increase in technological efficiency, the insidious process of overcultivation is persistently accelerated.

Although the Mossi recognize that different plants have different effects on the soil, they tend to attribute this as much to the differing consequences of the specific techniques required for the plants' cultivation as to the chemical action of the plants themselves. However they recognize the value of potash and phosphate and are aware of the usefulness of the green manures that release growth-promoting nitrates into the soil. They also recognize that crop rotation helps prevent any of the essential nutrients in the soil from being unduly exhausted.

To the extent that they are available, the Mossi make use of fertilizers. Animal excreta is used to increase soil fertility in several ways—by herding burros, goats, and sheep on the unused fields and, more importantly, by entering into a cooperative relationship with the Fulani pastoralists who herd their cattle on the fields during the months of the dry season. Mossi farmers frequently collect manure themselves, particularly the droppings of their burros, to spread on fields that they recognize to be particularly poor. The richer excreta of animals penned up and kept inactive during the growing season is also collected, but most of it is used for fertilizing the gardens.

Because the Mossi farmers do not use straw bedding for their penned animals, much rich liquid manure is lost. Chickens, usually allowed to run loose in the vicinity of the settlement, also make a contribution to the enrichment of the soil. However their droppings are not purposefully collected. The Mossi do not use human waste as fertilizer. However the latrine areas that surround every settlement are usually marked by luxuriant vegetation. And over the years, as communities shift their locations, some of this regenerated land is probably put back into cultivation.

Clearing and cleaning of the farmland, occasionally preceded by dry-season efforts at fertilization, is the first step in the cycle of activities associated with Mossi farming. Rudimentary attempts at further fertilization and at erosion control are followed by planting and weeding. The cycle ends with the harvest, transport, processing, and storage of the crop.

New land is cleared in April and early May, just at the end of the dry period. First, what remains of the grass and low underbrush of the previous rainy season is chopped out with a hoe or pulled up by hand and allowed to dry. Then it is set fire. Unburnt litter is collected into small piles and fired again. Valuable trees, such as the shea nut and baobab, are allowed to stand. The rest are purposefully destroyed by brush fires lit at the base of their trunks.

At this same time a part of a field with especially poor earth is occasionally fertilized with a mixture of manure and heavy loam from another field where a deeper topsoil has begun to form. Or, if the soil is thin in a particular area, it is sometimes laid over with a network of branches which holds the moisture and prevents further erosion when the rains begin, a technique that serves also to soften the topsoil for planting.

The use of the hoe to chop out old vegetation serves also to turn over the soil and prepare it for the planting which usually takes place after the first rains. In clearing and preparing the land for planting, the Mossi cultivator works bent over, chopping at the earth with the hoe in his right hand and collecting the sticks, stones, and other debris with his left. He uses his hoe to break up any large clods and then proceeds, transversing the field in a line, which separates the newly loosened soil from the unbroken earth. When hoeing is done in a group, the same sequence of actions carries the workers in a line across the field from side to side. Moving in unison and keeping abreast, they often work to the rhythm of a song.

After the rains have become more regular, usually in early June, the first cereals are planted. Most secondary crops are sown somewhat later, toward the end of June or early in July. In planting, the farmer bends forward, with the hoe in his right hand, making a scattering of slight depressions about eighteen inches apart. Three or four seeds taken from a gourd carrier are dropped into each shallow pocket which is then covered over with a final motion of the hoe.

Beans, peanuts, and other crops interplanted with cereals are not sown until after the first weeding of the fields, well past the time when the young millet stalks have begun to sprout. The utilization of the farmlands for the cultivation of more than a single crop has several advantages. By covering the soil they act as a control on erosion and as a means of inhibiting weed growth. Each plant uses different soil nutrients. Deep-rooted crops such as groundnuts help to open up and decompose the subsoil, and they are, of course, an important source of food and fodder. In turn, the larger crops of millet shade and protect the smaller plants until they get a start. Unfortunately, legumes—which are especially valuable as a crop for interplanting because of the nitrogen-fixing bacteria that form in their roots—are never used by the Mossi as green manure. They are not dug under when they are still juicy young plants that would decay rapidly, but are collected after picking and used as animal fodder. The immediate need for the beans and leaves as food for men and animals during the growing season prevents the gradual enrichment of the soil that would otherwise be effected by turning the plants under to decompose while still green.

Millet and sorghum fields are cultivated both by hand and with the hoe. The growth close to the base of the plant is pulled carefully by hand so as not to trample the dense interplanting of groundnuts or other crops. From time to time as he works, the farmer stops, knocks the dirt from the roots of the plants he has pulled up, and throws them onto the newly turned earth to wither and dry in the sun.

Mossi fields are cultivated between two and four times during the growing season, depending upon the availability of labor, the weather, and the industry of the individual farmer. The value of frequent weeding is recognized both as a means of weed control and of aerating and deepening the soil. But many farmers are unable to cultivate their fields as extensively as they would like because of the lack of labor. This shortage of workers results from the migration of the younger Mossi to Ghana and the Ivory Coast, where they often remain for several years.[3] Disease and the loss of energy caused by preharvest hunger are also factors that may influence the frequency with which fields can be worked.[4]

As their crops ripen, the farmers use a variety of techniques to protect them from predators—animal, human, and supernatural. To guard their fields from their own grazing animals and the few wild herbivores, they construct a barricade of sticks and brush. However, because this is only practicable if the field is relatively small, it is a technique used most often to protect fields of peanuts and tobacco located in the bush. Only exceptionally is it used for the protection of the larger fields of grain. Burros are tethered, and goats and sheep are herded away from the farmlands by the

3. The loss of the productive participation of Mossi youth in the traditional subsistence technology is probably considerable. To assess it properly it must be measured against the value of the money goods returned to Yatenga by the laborers. Most of this money is not used for investment, but is imported in the form of perishable consumer goods to be used in bridewealth payments. Such migration appears to contribute to the perpetuation of technological stagnation in Yatenga in two ways: by reducing the pressure for innovation in the traditional technology by providing an alternative means of acquiring money and consumer goods of foreign origin; and by draining the countryside of the potentially most productive segment of the labor force.

4. Although I have no adequate medical data on this question of the relation of physical conditions to work performance, it is clearly relevant. Two measures are needed: 1) the amount of time lost from farm work as the result of disease; 2) the decrease in work efficiency caused by illness or hunger.

children during the day. At night they are corralled. During the growing season the Fulani herdsmen take the cattle north of Yatenga, away from the farmlands entirely.

Later in the season children are frequently stationed in the fields to frighten off birds that threaten the crops. Often a thatch shelter is erected near the more distant fields where older boys remain at night to protect the newly ripened grain from thieves. This guard is strengthened when the grain is cut and piled temporarily in the fields before being carried back to the settlement for storage. During this time an anxious farmer sometimes sleeps on his farmlands himself, moving from field to field in a single night in an effort to baffle potential thieves from his own kin group who might otherwise calculate his nightly moves and plan their depredations accordingly.[5]

The first crop, inferior millet, is taken in sometime in August. The harvest of sorghum and cattail millet usually begins in November and lasts throughout the month. Cotton is picked beginning in September and continues to be gathered through January. Maize, peanuts, and beans are harvested from September to October.

The larger cereals are harvested with a straightedged knife. Bending down the stalk with his left hand, the harvester cuts a cluster of grain at the base of the head and then, with another slash lower down on the stalk, fells the plant. The panicles are collected into a large bunch and deposited on the ground. Later they are gathered, tied together in bundles about twenty inches in diameter, and stacked in a huge circular pile to dry for several days. After drying they are carried back to the household and stored in special granaries. The millet stalks themselves are left in the field to dry. Later, when the hard work of the harvest is over, the women and children return to gather them for kindling.

Each household head in the Mossi patriclan has separate granaries where he stores the cereals produced in his fields with the assistance of his wives and children. Other granaries, under the

5. There are also magical means of protecting fields from human and supernatural predators. These techniques, as well as the sacrifices designed to enrich the soil, to assure adequate rainfall, and to induce certain twin spirits to steal the "soul" from neighboring millet stands in order to enrich the harvest yields of their supplicants, are discussed along with other means of controlling the supernatural in Chapter 7.

"These earthen storehouses are of two types . . ."

proprietorship of the patriclan elder, contain the grain cultivated and harvested communally by the entire kin group. The head of each extended family also has a granary used for the storage of that part of the harvest produced as a result of the efforts of his family working as a unit. These earthen storehouses are of two types. The smaller one, where millet is stored after it has been threshed, has the appearance of a huge clay jar about six feet tall and four feet in circumference. Built on an eighteen-inch high foundation of stones and logs, its round walls come together at the top to form an aperture just large enough to permit the entry of a man. This top is capped with a small conical thatch roof. Unthreshed millet is stored in a larger granary, with a capacity of from twenty to thirty cubic feet, of the same basic construction, but with flat vertical walls set at right angles. One small window, just large enough to permit entry, is usually set high in the wall. This storehouse is covered with a conical roof of thatch.

Granaries made from woven mats attached together to form an enormous loosely fashioned basket, are set several feet off the ground on frameworks of crossed poles. These are used for storing peanuts, cotton, and smaller quantities of millet and sorghum which are usually kept in tightly woven baskets placed inside. They also are topped with conical roofs of thatch. Inferior millet is usually stored either in clay jars or in small earthen granaries kept inside the house. Corn is dried on the cob and hung in clusters under the eaves of the granaries.

The harvest yield of cereals in Yatenga is low in comparison with staple crops of rice, maize, and manioc grown elsewhere in West Africa. Of the two principal grains, the yield for sorghum appears to be somewhat greater. However the absence of adequate statistical data makes it difficult to give accurate figures for any of the agricultural products of Yatenga. Any estimate of an "average" yield must be qualified by a reminder of the variety of factors that may detract from its accuracy—a farmer's reluctance to reveal the full extent of his lands and harvests, variations in the quality of cultivation, differences in yield resulting from dissimilarities in the quality of seeds and soil, and, of course, yearly climatic variations. Given the fragility of the adjustment of the Mossi to their environment, it is to be expected that production figures would vary greatly from year to year. Thus, for example, an attack of malaria or

Guinea worm may interrupt, seriously retard, or prevent a man from preparing a field for planting, interfere with his doing the extensive weeding necessary for an abundant harvest, or result in damaging delays in getting his crops in on time. A hoe may break at the height of the planting season when a replacement can rarely be borrowed, and the smiths are themselves too busy in the fields to make quick repairs. Or a farmer may run out of seed and put off his planting until some can be borrowed or the money can be earned to purchase seed at inflated preharvest prices. A man may waken in the morning to find his older sons, his most valuable workers, have left secretly during the night to go south to Ghana and the Ivory Coast as migrant workers. Obtaining replacements for them is usually difficult. If he engages a cooperative work group or hires wage labor, it will be hard for him to control the quality of their work. Dissatisfaction on his part or theirs may result in quarrels and further delay.

Attention is given to these several sources of interference with the ideal progression of agricultural tasks because they help to explain what might otherwise appear to the observer to be a careless and disorganized approach to the conduct of farming endeavors. Given the Mossi's limited control over the many factors that affect his work, he must improvise to survive. The result is a schedule of activities and work performance—and a harvest—that are likely to fall far short of his aspirations.[6] And it is a rare and fortunate

6. I have not included any quantitative data on this subject because it is difficult in working among Mossi farmers to obtain representative samples. The harvest takes place during a few weeks. While I observed every phase of this activity, I did not have the facilities to take accurate measures ; nor is it likely that the farmers would have permitted this on a sufficiently extensive scale to collect data usable for analysis. To obtain such important information one would have to have a team of field assistants spread out over the community and any such effort would have to be preceded by a considerable campaign to win the confidence of the farmers. They would have every reason to assume that such information were being collected for the purpose of taxation.
A short monograph on the Mossi of Yatenga prepared under the aegis of the Service de l'Hydraulique de Haute-Volta (Izard-Heritier et Izard, 1959), presents some figures taken from an estimate of the harvests of seven families in the village of Touguin, but the authors themselves make it clear that such data are too limited to be of statistical value. The figures collected by the Service de l'Agriculture, Secteur de

farmer who is not beset by one or more of these troubles in a single season.

GARDENS

Most Mossi farmers keep gardens as a means of supplementing their food supply and of earning a small cash income. These are usually planted close to the family settlement unless the earth near the household and the wells has become too impoverished from long overcultivation. When gardens are nearby, they can be fertilized and watered more readily, and it is often possible to maintain them even during the dry season. Also it is easier to protect them from thieves. Garden soils are fertilized with a mixture of heavy loam and animal excreta. Droppings from the sheep and goats corralled inside the household dwellings are sometimes collected and spread to enrich the soil still further. Most gardens are enclosed by a low barrier of thorn brush which is cut and tied to a picket barrier of sticks. The Mossi do not make irrigation canals, but the soil around their garden plants is sometimes pushed up into hillocks, which are then depressed in the center to retain water. Large gardens and those located some distance from the compound residence are usually watered twice daily from a skin bucket. Smaller plots conveniently close to the house are watered sporadically, but more frequently, with water thrown out after cooking or washing.

Several varieties of indigenous tomato [koumba, red white, and bitter (Solanum incanum)], okra [mana (Hibiscus esculentus)], yellow yams [uya (Dioscorea cayenensis)], sweet potatoes [mwoso (Impomea patatas)], and manioc [bandakou (Manihot utilissima)] are the vegetables most frequently cultivated in Mossi gardens. Gourds are grown as food containers. In addition to these, such nonindigenous vegetables as onions, eggplant, and a European

Ouahigouya are, I believe, equally unreliable, both because of the difficulty of getting the cooperation of the Mossi for this sort of enquiry under the best of circumstances and the fact that such government agencies were generally ineffective in communicating with the Mossi. They always got their figures, but the extent to which such figures were a reflection of reality is open to serious question. As a result I have felt it would be misleading to utilize them here.

"Most gardens are enclosed by a low barrier of thorn brush . . ."

variety of tomato are extensively cultivated. Most of these garden crops are used in the preparation of the highly seasoned sauces which are served with millet cakes or porridge. Chili peppers [kiparey (Capiscum frutescent)] and sorrel [bi (Hibiscus sabdarifa)]. the principal condiments, are frequently grown as garden crops. Tobacco also is often cultivated by Mossi gardeners.

Gardens are planted and cultivated with the same tools used in the fields. Because the plots are less extensive and are often more densely interplanted, they are usually weeded entirely by hand. Some plants, such as tomatoes, eggplant, and tobacco, are separated and usually reset as seedlings in the garden, but sometimes they are replanted in the fields where millet and sorghum grow.

Techniques of harvesting garden produce vary, of course, with each plant. Tomatoes and eggplant are picked and consumed or marketed as soon as they ripen. The leaves of the eggplant are often boiled and left to dry in the sun, after which they are stored in clay jars. To obtain seeds, some tomatoes and eggplants are skewered, dried, and stored in the rafters inside the house. Okra is harvested with a small knife and is either consumed at once or left to dry. Yams and sweet potatoes are usually harvested from September to January. Although they are ready to be eaten by early fall, they are frequently left for several months in the ground, which dries out quickly once the rains have ceased. Otherwise they are harvested and stored in shallow holes dug near the household dwelling. Tobacco leaves are cut off as they ripen, a process which begins in September. The leaves are tied to the house rafters to dry or are spread out in the courtyard. When free of moisture, they are pounded and mixed with freshly cut green tobacco leaves, molded into a ball about three inches in circumference, and dried again; they are then ready to be stored in clay jars kept inside the house.

Many of the crops grown in the fields, such as millet, sorghum, and peanuts, are also cultivated in small garden plots near the settlement or sometimes within it, planted in a single row beside a house or along the wall of a courtyard where they can be readily fertilized and watered from the kitchen. Although neither garden crops nor the techniques by which they are cultivated are absolutely distinct from farm products and the procedures by which they are cultivated, Mossi gardens are always more intensively worked.[7,8]

DOMESTIC ANIMALS

Cattle are most important among the domestic animals of the Mossi. Usually, however, they do not tend them themselves, but assign them to Fulani herdsmen. The symbiotic tie the Mossi enjoy with the Fulani herdsmen represents a further dimension of the complex adjustment to the natural environment achieved by the peoples of Yatenga. The climatic conditions of the region are equally suited to pastoral nomadism which is widespread. The distinctive technologies of the two groups, the Mossi farmers and the Fulani herdsmen, are so organized that they complement one another to use fully if not most productively nearly every aspect of the natural environment.

The Fulani herdsmen who live throughout Yatenga for part of the year tend the Mossi cattle in exchange for their milk and a portion of their young and for the right to camp on the Mossi farms and to receive occasional gifts of millet to supplement their diet of milk and cheese. During the dry season they graze their herds on the unused farmlands of their Mossi hosts, providing a valued means of enriching the soil. Occasionally the Fulani are granted the right to use a little land for the cultivation of some millet of their own, an operation conducted unenthusiastically and ineptly

7. This creates a problem in nomenclature. In anthropology the term *horticulture* has usually been used to refer to less effective or efficient techniques of food growing. The exclusive use of handtools; the absence of fertilizers and of crop rotation and fallowing; and ignorance of irrigation are usually implied—all factors conducive to lower productivity. Agriculture, on the other hand, is a term that has been reserved for more efficient techniques of food growing. Neither term works very well for the Mossi. For in many ways the techniques they use in gardening, the "horticultural" aspect of their subsistence technology, are more efficient than the techniques used on their farms.

8. Mossi gardens also have a different economic role: Their maintenance is usually an individual enterprise. For the women who frequently keep them, gardens are one of the few legitimate means of earning money. Often they are used to raise a small cash crop of peanuts or cotton in addition to the vegetables grown for the kitchen.

by Fulani women. Most of the herdsmen are permanently nomadic, others remain settled for one or more seasons on the outskirts of a Mossi village. Frequently these settlements are inhabited constantly over the years by a succession of such temporarily sedentary Fulani groups. But even when they remain settled for several years, cattle keeping necessarily continues to be their principal concern. Whatever farmland they are ceded is usually so poor and they work it so badly that they must sell some of their cattle to purchase the additional millet needed to get them through the year.

In addition to their occasional and always desultory work in the fields, the Fulani women are charged with milking and the preparation of the curds and butter which they mold into small round pats and sell in the market, using the money to buy garden vegetables, condiments, cloth, and the simple utensils necessary to maintain their meagre households.

As the rains begin and the farmlands must be cleared and cleaned for planting, the Fulani herdsmen take their cattle, and those belonging to their Mossi hosts, and move slowly northward where the increasing rains bring grass to the southern fringes of the Sahara.

The Mossi cattle serve as a means of storing wealth and as a source of prestige. They provide the principal means of cash investment available within the context of the traditional economy. Cattle are rarely slaughtered for food, and then only by wealthy men on important ceremonial occasions. When cattle sicken, they are killed, and their skin is used to make shoes, bags and buckets, saddlery and cord. Their horns often serve as salt containers.

All other domestic animals are tended by the Mossi themselves. During the dry months their burros are occasionally hobbled near the household and allowed to graze. Toward the end of the dry season, when the land has been grazed clean, they are fed on forage collected after the previous harvest. When the rains begin, burros are kept permanently inside the settlement compound and taken out only occasionally to be watered or used for transport to a distant field. Fresh grass is gathered by the children and carried in to them each day. Burros are used principally as pack animals, for personal transport, and as a means of storing wealth. They are killed for food only when they fall sick or have grown too old to be

"... Fulani herdsmen ... tend the Mossi cattle in exchange for their milk and a portion of their young ..."

useful. Their skins are crudely tanned and used as the coverings for sleeping mats.

Horses are of even less significance in Mossi technology. However they have an economic role of some importance. Only the chiefs and a few of the elders of wealthy lineages keep them; they serve principally as a repository of value and as a means of conspicuous display. Sometimes they are ridden short distances on ceremonial occasions, but most often they are used in exhibition races, when they are covered with elaborate leatherwork and wood saddlery and used by their riders to demonstrate their prowess as horsemen and their status as men of wealth. Horses are rarely grazed, but are usually kept tethered on display just outside the entrance to their owner's residence. During the dry season they are fed with forage collected and stored after the previous harvest. They are also given millet. In the rainy months fresh grass is cut for them each day by the children. The Mossi eat their horses only when they sicken or die of old age. Their hide is not utilized. Only their tails are kept to be made into fly switches.

Goats are left to find their own feed during the dry months. They are released during the day in the care of the children of the family who herd them on the farmlands. In the evening they are watered at the well and penned up in small, mud-walled corrals inside the household settlement. Once the rains begin they are kept there during the day also. Or, occasionally, they are taken by their small herdsmen into parts of the bush where there is no danger of their damaging the crops. Goats are kept for their meat and milk and they also serve as a means of storing wealth. They are frequently given as marriage presents. When killed, a portion of their carcass is usually sold in the market. Their skins are used in making water-bags, and thongs for sandals and as floor coverings.

Sheep are tended in the same manner, but are kept only for their meat and hide, because their wool is too scanty to be of value. Pigs, which must root for themselves in the dry months, are also closed inside the residence at night. During the rainy season they are kept penned up permanently and are fed on forage.

Chickens roost at night in crudely constructed coops made of sticks, but run freely about the settlement during the day. What they find for themselves in the way of food is supplemented by corn and millet given them by their owners each evening. Chickens are kept in greater abundance than other domestic animals and are most often killed when an important occasion justifies the addition of a meat dish to the usual Mossi daily fare of porridge and vegetables. They are also most often used in sacrifice. The Guinea fowl kept by the Mossi roost in trees inside the residence or in coops similar to those used for chickens. They are kept also for their meat. Although not used for sacrifices, Guinea fowl are given frequently as gifts or used as payment for work. Few ducks are kept by the Mossi because of the scarcity of permanent rivers, streams, or ponds. Considered a luxury food, they are consumed only by the wealthy. Pigeons, also rare in Yatenga, are kept in special roosts built in the roofs of the granaries and are fattened on millet and corn.

Dogs are used as household guards, as scavengers, and in the hunt. Although not a prestige food, they are frequently killed and eaten when they begin to get old. Also they are often sold to traders who take them south to market among the Gourounsi who regard them as more appetizing fare. Cats are occasionally kept as scavengers and to protect the granaries from mice.

Bees are domesticated. Hives, in the form of elongated straw cylinders, are kept in trees. Children extract the honey about once a month using a torch to control the insects. It is eaten as it comes from the hive or is mixed with milk or millet gruel. Beeswax is sold to the smiths who use it in jewelry making; it is also used by leather-workers for softening hides.

GATHERING

Gathering is a persistently important aspect of the subsistence technology of the Mossi, a further dimension of the near total utilization they make of their environment. Although it is a task formally assigned to women and children, anyone who encounters wild food collects it to eat on the spot or to take home to add to the family pot. Every Mossi recognizes the variety of useful wild seeds, fruits, leaves, and bark available in the bush. With the exception of a few papaya, mango, and baobab trees which in recent years have been purposefully planted, the Mossi do not plant or cultivate the trees that grow in their homeland, but they do rely importantly on their products. The fruit of the shea nut [*tanga (Butyrospermum parkii)*], is perhaps the most greatly valued and widely utilized of all wild fruits. Gathered as it ripens, from June to December, it is taken from the trees by women and children and collected in baskets. The outer meat, which has a sweet taste, is sometimes eaten immediately, but most of the fruit is placed intact in large jars and left to ferment for several months. Then, after further processing, it serves as cooking oil and as a staple ingredient in vegetable sauces.

The leaves of the baobab [*twega (Adansonia digitata)*] are gathered to be used either fresh or dried in the preparation of the sauce called *twega ziedo*, which is an almost daily item in the Mossi menu from June to October, when the tree is in leaf. Fibers taken from the trunk and, less often, the roots of the tree are used to make cord. The tallest baobab are also used as lookout posts in searching for stray animals or as vantage points from which important public announcements are made. Before the European conquest these trees also served as sentinel posts in warfare.

The fruit of the tamarind [*poussogo (Tamarindus indica)*], valued as one of the few fruits available during the dry season, is collected by the women from February until May. The long brown pods are stripped of their outer skin, and the fruit pulp is mashed and rolled into balls about the size of an orange and then stored, sold in the market, or added to the family menu. Tamarind leaves are used as a seasoning in cooking. The fruit of the Jujubier [*mugunugu (Ziziphus jujuba)*] is gathered in February. About the size of a pea, it is pounded and dried before eating. Both the fruit and the wood of the fig tree [*kakanga (Ficus gnaphalocarpa)*] are utilized by the Mossi. Often the fruit is eaten raw, and the wood is much used for fire making. The liana [*wedega (Landolphia senegalensis)*] provides a small bitter fruit which is squeezed to produce a sour juice sometimes added to the water used for drinking and cooking. Branches of the tree serve to make lightweight cord. The scrub acacia [*karadiga (Acacia macrostachya)*] produces a small, tasteless fruit gathered as a source of bulk in the preparation of sauces. The large green fruit of a tree the Mossi call *mobogo (Poupartia birrea)* looks much like an unripe mango. Gathered in June, its outer skin is removed to expose a grainy-textured inner fruit which is boiled to make a liquid flavoring used in sauces. Once prepared it is stored in clay jars.

"The leaves of the baobab tree are gathered to be used in the preparation of a sauce called *Twega ziedo* . . . an almost daily item on the Mossi menu."

Other trees whose fruits are gathered by the Mossi include the
*silingore (Capparis corymbosa), mapagoba zoukongo (Grevia
flavescent), cansalaga (Bridelia tenuifoylia), byeghella (Balinetis
aegyptiaca), dabaga (Ampelocissus grantii), sougada (Cassia tora),
dito (Hibiscus sabdarifa)*, and the flowers and leaves of the *gunga
(Bombax pantandrum)*.⁹ Many of these leaves and fruits are
gathered for medicinal purposes. Yaws, for example, are treated
with a liquid obtained from boiling the leaves of the pulverized bark
of the tamarind. The fruit of the liana is used in draughts prepared
to protect the eyes from the damaging effects of measles, and the
roots of the jujubier are employed in the preparation of a cure
for colic.¹⁰

In addition to the regular Mossi fare, there are a number of
plants gathered extensively only during periods of famine. They
include the leaves of a small tree [*nyadiga (Vitex cuneata)*], a wild
grass [*uda (Dactylonum eagyptum)*], a stalky weed [*koussouga
(Seteria pallidifusca)*], the seeds of a grass ordinarily gathered as
animal forage [*kalaniango (Elinnorus elegans)*], the roots of the
kidba plant *(Stylochitron hypogaeus)*, and the bulb of the *senga*
shrub *(Curculigo pilosa)*.

The base of trees bearing edible fruits is sometimes protected
from scavengers by an enclosure of thorn branches put up by the
proprietor of the field in which they stand. Otherwise no special
techniques are employed in gathering. The only tools used are
simple fiber baskets, gourds, leather containers, and occasionally
a small knife.

Among the minerals collected by the Mossi, water is, of course,
the most important. It is obtained from streams, rivers, pools that
form during the rainy season, and wells. Mossi wells are deep, often
descending as much as seventy meters. Most well-holes are un-
protected above ground. Thus, they receive the highly unsanitary
waters that run off the surrounding earth which is muddied by the
overflow from buckets and the water used in washing clothes—or
sores, especially yaws and Guinea worm lesions. A skin bucket
attached to a rope made of twisted fiber is used to draw water. Some

9. A complete list would obviously be much longer. However, as
far as I know, a thorough study of Mossi pharmacopoeia has not yet
been made.
10. See A. Prost (1941, pp. 55–56).

European buckets are also employed, but usually they are quickly battered to pieces from striking the rough and often rocky inner sides of the well. Once drawn, the water is poured into large clay jars and carried back to the household. Earth with a high saline content is the only other mineral purposefully extracted by the Mossi for human consumption. Occasionally salt formed in small surface pans is eaten by pregnant women and by children and animals.[11] With the exception of iron ore, no other minerals are extracted from the subsoils of Yatenga; apparently they are as poor in exploitable potential as the thin sandy surface soils seem to be.

HUNTING

Hunting is less important than gathering as an aspect of Mossi technology because there is so little game. Nutritionally small animals and insects are probably most important in the diet of young children for whom hunting frogs and lizards is a form of play. For adult men hunting is primarily of importance as recreation and as a means of reinforcing the solidarity of certain social groups and their allegiance to certain religious and political leaders.[12]

Antelope and rabbits, the principal game, are usually hunted by groups of five to ten men accompanied by their dogs. But several times a year larger hunts are organized in which as many as fifty or sixty men participate. The kill from a hunt of either sort is rarely abundant enough to constitute an important addition to the food supply. Although the Mossi have bows, arrows, and spears, they rarely use them. They say they have lost their skill with these weapons because they can no longer be used in warfare. Instead they hunt with slingshots and sticks and stones, running down their wounded prey and beating it to death. Meat is usually cut up and boiled by the women. Occasionally small pieces are attached to a fire-hardened stick and roasted directly over the flames. Meat is most often served as part of a sauce eaten with millet cakes or porridge.

11. The rock salt which is an important item in Mossi diet is obtained through the market where it is most often sold by traders from Mali.
12. These more important, but nontechnological, aspects of the hunt are discussed in Chapter 8.

Fishing, it has been noted, is impossible in most parts of Yatenga because of the scarcity of permanent streams or lakes. However the markets usually have a supply of dried or smoked fish imported from the river city of Mopti in central Mali.

Everyone hunts flying termites and locusts which periodically invade Yatenga. The Mossi trap them by building fires under the trees where they settle at night. Partially suffocated by the smoke, they fall to the ground where they are collected and usually roasted and eaten immediately.

FOOD PREPARATION

Most Mossi foods are prepared with millet. Cakes, porridge, and gruel prepared with millet or sorghum flour as their basic ingredient, and served with a variety of vegetable and meat sauces and garnishes, are the most recurrent items.

Of the several implements used in food preparation, the largest is the grinding platform, *nere,* a low, circular structure made of mud bricks about three feet high and varying from fifteen to twenty feet in diameter. The surface of the platform is made rainproof with a mixture of ashes, dung, and lateritic dust which is beaten by the women with small paddles until it is almost as hard as cement. A small patriclan residence usually has a single grinding platform which is used by all the women. Larger dwellings sometimes have several such platforms.

Before it is ground, the grain is pounded with a wooden mortar and pestle of a type used widely throughout West Africa. Both implements are made by the smiths. Other wooden utensils used in the kitchen include small bowls, also made by the smiths, and a variety of calabashes used for winnowing, as containers for millet porridge and sauce, and as dippers and drinking cups. A tray made of woven straw is used with the calabashes to winnow the pounded grain. Containers used for cooking are of several types. Millet cakes and porridge are prepared in a pot approximately thirty centimeters in diameter. A slightly smaller pot is used for the preparation of sauces. Beer is made in huge brewing jars about forty centimeters in diameter.

Each woman cooks in an area of the courtyard adjacent to her own dwelling. A few stones on which the pots are set, a small pile

"Each woman cooks in an area of the courtyard adjacent to her own individual dwelling."

of sticks and dried brush for kindling, and ashes and charred pieces of wood usually mark the spot. Most women have a flat stone or low wooden stool on which they sit while cooking. A clay water jar, a stick for stirring, a straw sieve, a broken piece of matting for fanning the fire, and a knife complete the Mossi woman's collection of kitchen equipment.

Ordinarily grain is taken from the storehouse and threshed only when it is needed for cooking. The clumps of millet or sorghum are first laid out on a freshly swept area of hardened earth and then beaten with a stick or the branches of a tree. They are then pounded in the wooden mortar and winnowed by pouring from one calabash or tightly woven basket container to another. According to the most common method of preparing flour, the pounded grains are further pulverized on the grinding stone with a small stone *(nebilo)* which is rolled back and forth over them until they are reduced to flour. By another method the millet is moistened before pounding in the mortar. After winnowing, the damp grain is soaked in water until it swells and then pounded a second time to attain a heavy flour which, after sifting, is ready to cook.

Flour prepared by either method is used to make *sacabo,* a millet cake which is the basic staple in the Mossi diet. The juice from the leaves of the tamarind tree is first boiled with water. Then millet flour is added to form a paste which is cooked until it reaches the consistency of a very thick porridge. It is served with a variety of leafy sauces spiced with peppers. Millet flour is also used in the preparation of fritters which are cooked rapidly in boiling water, dipped in raw flour, and served coated with shea butter and seasoned with salt and pepper.

A moist dough of ground peanuts mixed with cooked millet flour and pounded to a porridge-like consistency is another common preparation. Other basic dishes made with millet include a small pancake and dumplings made with a mixture of millet flour and cotton seed.

Flour made from sorghum or inferior millet is processed and cooked using the same techniques. Because maize is one of the first cereals to be harvested, some of it is often roasted on the cob and eaten immediately, but most of the crop is stored. The dried kernels are made into flour by the same methods used for millet and sorghum. A cakelike porridge made with maize flour is served, as are millet cakes, with a variety of vegetable sauces. In another dish the whole kernels of maize are removed from the cob and boiled with beans and salt. For infants and old people unable to take solid food, the kernels are scraped from the cob after roasting and ground to make a soft paste.

Dried beans are usually cooked with water, millet ash, and pepper to make a vegetable stew. Sometimes they are soaked, ground, and cooked to the consistency of a cake, mixed with rice, and served boiled or prepared as fritters.

Most of the leaves of trees and shrubs the Mossi gather to make sauces and vegetable garnishes are prepared by boiling in earthen jars. In some instances millet, corn flour, or cotton seeds are added to the boiling mixture to give it body, after which it may be consumed as a single dish. But more often the leaves are prepared as part of a sauce. One made with the leaves of the baobab is the most common. It can be prepared with fresh or dried leaves, which are first pounded in a mortar until they form a paste and then mixed with fermented sorrel seeds and water drained from the ash of millet cakes and salt. The sauce is cooked for about two hours, after which meat is often added and cooked in the sauce for another two hours before serving.

This same general procedure is followed in the preparation of other sauces. The principal vegetable ingredients in Mossi sauces vary with the seasonal availability of different greens. Sauces are also made with a base of cotton, mimosa, or sesame seeds. Some are enriched with the addition of a thick paste of ground peanuts.

Chicken is the meat the Mosssi eat most frequently, but even it is consumed only on rare and important occasions. Normally it is cut up and boiled into a stew, to which shea butter, salt, and pepper are added. Goat meat and mutton and pork are prepared in the same manner. The Mossi prefer beef, but it is usually too costly. However when beef is prepared it is fixed in much the same way— cut up and boiled, or occasionally skewered on a stick and grilled. Fish, either dried or smoked, is first soaked until soft and then boiled with onions, peppers, and salt. Frogs are first dried and then pounded and added to any vegetable sauce. Termites may be included in the same way, but are also fried with millet ash. Locusts are often simply held by the wings over an open fire and quickly roasted and eaten on the spot as a sort of hors d'oeuvre.

Zom kom, a thin gruel of water and millet flour, is the principal nonalcoholic beverage of the Mossi. The drink most often offered to guests, it is used also as a sacrificial libation. The juices of the fruits of the *Lannoa microcarpa, Poupartia birrea,* and *Tamarindus indica* are frequently added to water and drunk either hot or cold. Beer, *ram,* is prepared from millet or sorghum boiled with water and set with yeast to ferment. Although it has only a mild alcoholic content, it is served usually by the calabash and in sufficient quantities to induce at least mild intoxication. Honey is sometimes added and a longer period of fermentation is allowed in order to produce a somewhat stronger brew. Beer is stored in clay jars which when set in the wind keep their contents cool.

In addition to salt, which is usually purchased in the market, the Mossi use fermented sorrel seeds, potassium made from water in which millet ash has been dissolved, tamarind juice, and peanut oil as condiments. Kola nuts, the principal excitant used by the Mossi, are not grown in Yatenga; they are imported by migrant laborers returning from the Guinea forest or are purchased in the market. Serving both as a stimulant and as a mask for hunger and fatigue, they are offered frequently to guests, exchanged often between friends, and consumed individually throughout the day.

A man distributes millet from his granaries every few days. If he has several wives, each should receive a share that may vary with the number of her children but should otherwise be equal to what her fellow co-wives receive. The wife is expected to prepare two cooked meals a day, one at midmorning and the other early in the evening. A woman fixes food for herself and her children and for her husband, unless he has several wives and the task is shared. In polygamous households friendly co-wives often cooperate in the preparation of their husband's meal. If relations are less amicable, they take turns. The morning meal usually consists of cold millet cakes left over from the night before and a calabash of flour and water. Toward the end of the growing season, when millet stores are running low, this meal is sometimes replaced by a few groundnuts taken hastily with water before departure for the fields. At sundown a heavier meal of millet cakes, vegetables, and sometimes a little meat is served. Men and women eat separately, the men with their male kinsmen, either those belonging to their own minimal lineage or, if the compound residence is small, with all the male members of the patriclan.

Food is carried out to them by their wives, who must kneel to place it before them with deference. Seated on mats or squatting on the ground, the men cluster around the food to form a circle. They eat with their right hands, tearing off a piece of millet cake and dipping it into the sauce with cupped fingers. Calabashes of water are passed about by their sons. There is little conversation. Those who have finished leave the group or turn their backs until the others have ended their meal, for it is considered rude to watch another while he eats or to engage him in conversation.

Infants are fed small pieces of millet cake dipped in sauce as soon as they can take solid food. By the time they are eighteen months old, they are usually able to feed themselves easily, and by three or four they have begun to hunt for the insects and rodents they cook over their own tiny fires. Babies and very young children are frequently fed by their fathers or grandfathers, often while sitting on their laps. Girls take their food with their male kinsmen only when they are very small, and then only occasionally. Once they begin to walk, they must join their mothers and sisters. Older boys, who wait on their elders during the meal, eat only when the others have finished. Women eat in the kitchens with their daughters and, occasionally, their co-wives or their husbands' mothers.

CRAFTS

All the Mossi are farmers—chiefs, Earth priests, blacksmiths, women, children, and the aged as well. During the growing season all except the sick, infants, the very old, and the very, very important must work on the farms. Only when the rains have stopped and the harvest is in can they turn their attention to more specialized activities such as metalworking, pottery making, basketry, weaving, carpentry, and house building—all tasks important to their material well-being, but less critical than the production of food itself.

Metallurgy

The working of metal and wood and the manufacture of pottery, the most specialized of Mossi crafts, are almost exclusively confined to the smiths, *saba,* who form an endogamous caste descended

from the indigenous inhabitants of Yatenga. Some iron ore is still
taken from caves dug by the smiths into the sides of the ferruginous
hills that are a typical aspect of the landscape and smelted in clay
furnaces located nearby. The ore is then run off into pits and
allowed to cool, broken up with a mallet, and carried back to the
settlement to be stored. Today, however, most iron used by Mossi
smiths is obtained from European sources.

Metal is worked over a charcoal fire built in front of a double
bellows made of sheepskin or goatskin. The red-hot ore is beaten
into shape on an anvil which is pointed on the underside so it can
be steadied by the hand or thrust into the ground. Metalworking
tools include the iron mallet, tongs, hammer, rasp, and a variety
of wedges used to make designs. With these tools the smiths make
the iron heads for hoes and hammers as well as swords, knives,
spears, arrow points, and needles.

Metal jewelry is usually fashioned from copper, zinc, or brass.
Both rings and bracelets are made by the lost-wax process. First
the circumference of the ring or bracelet is measured with string.
Then a wax mold is made and coated with clay which, when it
hardens, is plunged into boiling water to remove the wax. The
molten metal is then poured into the tubular form. Next the piece
is embellished with designs made with a file, chisel, or wedge.
Finally it is held over the fire with tongs and reheated, and the
ends are drawn together to encircle the wearer's finger or wrist.
Bracelets and rings are also made of twisted copper and zinc or
brass wire. The elaborate headstall, bit, and sharply pointed metal
spurs used by horsemen are also manufactured by the smiths. All
these tasks are undertaken only after the crops are in; during the
rainy months the smiths make only emergency repairs, and these
grudgingly.

Carpentry

Mossi smiths are also woodworkers. Mortars and pestles, bowls,
small stools, and wooden doors are the principal items in their
repertoire. An axe or adze, a knife, and a hatchet are the tools they
use. The low wooden stools they carve are often made to resemble
four-footed animals, frequently turtles or crocodiles. Aside from
these stools, the Mossi have no furniture. They sit on the floor,

"Metal is worked over a charcoal fire built in front of a double bellows . . ."

either on a mat or on their haunches. They take their meals seated in a squatting position, and they sleep on mats. Their personal belongings are now sometimes kept in small wooden chests made by European-trained carpenters, but traditionally such goods were wrapped in cloth and suspended from the rafters inside the house, a place well protected from the termites that are liable to attack any articles of wood or cloth left lying for long on the ground or on the earthen floor.

The doors used to close Mossi houses are made from three rough-hewn planks, about three and one half feet in length. The planks are fastened together with two smaller transverse boards and closed with carved, intricately constructed wooden locks which are fitted with iron keys also produced by the smiths. But many houses have mats to cover entrances and no doors at all.

Pottery

The wives of the smiths are potters. Using earth mixed with the crushed fragments of discarded pots, they turn the small containers used in cooking and serving food and in the preparation of beer and for storage on a clay wheel. After drying, the pots are fired in pits dug in the ground. These are first dusted with dry powder. Then the wet pottery is placed inside and packed around with straw, twigs, and pieces of bark which are then set fire. The pots are baked for about twelve hours. Then they are removed and, after cooling, immersed in larger earthen vessels filled with water and the crushed bark of a certain tree *(Poupartia birrea)* which imparts a reddish sheen to the finished vessel. Just as their husbands' metal-working and woodworking, the wives' pottery making is confined to the months of the dry season.

Basketry

Basketry, a specialized craft, can be practiced by anyone able to learn it. Mossi baskets, made from straw obtained from a variety of wild grasses, are often dyed black by immersion in the dark earth of stream beds or red by boiling in vessels filled with water and the crushed stalks of sorghum. Large, flat, straw trays, sleeping mats, and mats used as a replacement for wooden doors are made

"They use a wooden loom, *kaura,* of a type found throughout the Western Sudan."

using a coarser weave and thicker fibers. The only special tool used in basketry is a heavy iron needle made by the smiths, which is used to stitch the baskets together with hemp thread.

Leatherworking

Sandals, pouches, satchels, bags used to hold water and grain, sheathes for knives and swords, saddles and bridles, and the covering for amulets are the principal products of the leather-workers. Sheepskin and goatskin are used more frequently than cowhide. Leather is first soaked and then scraped and beaten with a stick or kneaded until it is soft. Then it is sometimes rubbed with butter. Finally it is cut and scraped with a regular knife and sewn with an awl. Afterwards, designs are imprinted with a variety of small iron stamps.

Textiles

Weaving and tailoring are also somewhat specialized tasks, but most adult men know how to weave the cotton thread spun by their wives and how to sew it into garments. They use a wooden loom, kuara, of a type found throughout the Western Sudan. Often the warp and woof are of different colors, with blue and red most frequently providing the contrast with the natural color of the cotton. Strips of cloth and even completed garments are sometimes dyed in the indigo vats found in every village. Dyeing is a special-ized craft, but can be undertaken by any male. Although most men make their own garments if locally woven cotton is to be used, cloth of European manufacture is usually sewn by tailors on the antiquated sewing machines now a part of every large Mossi market.

Shelter

Every Mossi compound dwelling, saka, is comprised of the individual houses of its inhabitants, each with its own courtyard. The entire compound structure is surrounded by a mud brick wall about four feet high. The construction of the one-room Mossi house, zaka, and its adjacent walled courtyard, the sun shelters, the granaries, and the grinding platforms that comprise the compound dwelling involve skills all Mossi adults possess and use.

"Every Mossi compound dwelling is comprised of the numerous individual houses of its inhabitants, each with its own courtyard."

The typical round Mossi house has a diameter of about ten feet. Its circular walls, about five feet high, are topped with a conical thatched roof approximately three feet high at the center. There are no windows and only one small door. At the place where the house is to be constructed, a circle is first traced on the ground, using a compass made from a stick and a piece of string. Around this a wall of bricks made of earth mixed with straw and millet husks is constructed, each layer being secured with a thin spread of moist earth. Only two or three rows of bricks are laid in a single day, to allow for thorough drying and settling. After drying, the exterior of the walls is rubbed with a mixture of earth, cinders, and dung which has the consistency of stucco and is somewhat water repellent. This same mixture is laid down in several layers and beaten with a small wooden paddle to make the floor of the house and the courtyard. The door is cut when the wallls are completed.

The roof of the house is constructed on the ground. First a conical frame is made of branches fastened together with fiber cord. Over this, two layers of straw are placed in spiral, overlapping rows and lashed to the wooden frame with more cord. Then the roof is set on top of the house. Weapons, tools, and other small possessions are tied to the underside of the roof frame to weight it. The door of the house usually faces on a courtyard used for cooking which is formed by the construction of a semicircular wall about the same height as the walls of the house and joined on to the sides of the adjacent houses and courtyards of other inhabitants of the compound residence.

The other principal structure typical of the Mossi compound dwelling is much simpler. This is the thatch-covered sun shelter, *zande,* where the men of the lineage take their meals, rest, and work at the repair of their weapons and tools. The roof of this shelter is often used as a drying platform for forage and as a storage place for tools, weapons, and containers. Varying in area from fifty to two hundred and fifty square feet, the shelter is formed by a number of slender poles driven into the ground at intervals of about four feet and covered over with a flat, loose framework of lighter sticks to which straw mats are secured with fiber cord. This shelter is used principally in the dry period. During the growing season, when farmers are away in their fields for most of the day, the mats that form the roof are removed and stored to protect them from the rains.

Apprenticeship

The skills involved in almost all aspects of Mossi technology are acquired within the kin group. Because craft specializations not determined by caste affiliation are practiced within every patriclan, there is no apprenticeship system outside the family. Within it instructions are informally organized and based on reciprocity. The young man who wishes to learn the special skills of an elder can request permission to assist him. Or a man may ask for the aid of a younger kinsman in exchange for teaching him his skills. He shares with the apprentice a portion of the profits from their joint endeavor. Generally children are encouraged to assist their elders and to observe all their activities with care.

But in accordance with a Mossi tradition which tends to inhibit direction in communication, especially between persons of differing status, young people are not encouraged to ask questions about the tasks they seek or are required to learn. Their queries are discouraged, first with silence, then, if they persist, with a ridiculous answer, and finally with a threat or a blow which usually drives the child off and ends the lesson. This attitude, which permeates the Mossi educational system, has a serious effect on the accumulation and transmission of experience necessary for technological advance. Lessons are never formal. Questions asked are rarely answered, and, of course, because the Mossi are illiterate there is no means of permanently recording experience. To an extent, perhaps, this is compensated for by the encouragement the young people receive to participate in the activities of their elders. But it is doubtful that this is enough. Much of value must be lost.

TRANSPORT AND COMMUNICATIONS

The Mossi carry most things on their heads. Their feet are their principal means of transport. And messages can only be communicated by word of mouth.

Although Mossi keep cattle and horses, burros are the only animals used regularly for transport. Cattle are never ridden or used as pack animals. Horses are used exclusively for riding, and then only on ceremonial occasions; the Mossi regard them, correctly, as being very delicate and hard to care for. Their horses are not hardy enough to be used as pack animals nor fast enough to provide a useful alternative to walking as a means of human transport. Today most Mossi who can afford to do so travel by bicycle or truck. However distances of several hundred miles are still frequently covered by foot.

Burros are often used as pack animals and for human transport. They are ridden without a saddle, with the rider seated well back on the animal's rump. Riders whose legs are longer than their small mounts are tall must hold their legs carefully out to the sides to keep them from brushing the ground. Burros are ordinarily used only for transport where the distance is relatively great—to travel to farmlands located a long way from the settlement, to carry firewood collected deep in the bush, or to take goods to market in another village.

The Mossi have several small drums used on ceremonial occasions to reproduce the tones that represent proverbs or to announce the arrival of the chief. Although these work on the same principle as the talking drums used elsewhere in Africa, particularly in the Congo, the Mossi do not otherwise use them as a means of communication.

The Mossi had no indigenous form of writing and are almost universally illiterate in French, the official language. Knowledge of written Arabic is almost entirely confined to the infrequent copying of sacred texts. Although *möré* has been phonetically transcribed by missionaries, only a handful of Mossi Protestants are literate; and all they have to read are the Bible and a few awkward transcriptions of Mossi proverbs. Consequently communications within the community and between communities can only be carried verbally.

In short, transport and communications are scarcely developed beyond the local area. But, within the context of the traditional technology, it is only there that they are needed.

Natural conditions in Yatenga are harsh. The soil is poor and most of the time there is not enough water, or for short periods there is often too much. It is almost always too hot for comfort. Game is scarce, and there is much disease. Protein deficiency is chronic.

". . . burros are the only animals used regularly for transport."

Even though they are often sick or hungry, the Mossi work hard nearly all the time. They make a living, but they never "get ahead."

The nature of their environment and of their technological adjustment to it clearly affects in important ways the development of the other institutions of their culture, especially their economic organization.

CHAPTER FOUR

ECONOMIC ORGANIZATION

Essentially three things need to be understood about the operation of the economic system of the Mossi: the way they allocate productive goods, the way they organize themselves for work, and the way they organize the distribution of the products of their work.

PRODUCTIVE GOODS

For the farmers of Yatenga, land is obviously the basic productive good. The Mossi concept of land embodies a variety of specific meanings. The generic term *tenga* is used for the earth, the village, the Earth shrine, and sometimes for the entire Mossi community. In a sense all the land belongs to all the Mossi, to their gods, to their ancestral spirits, and to the generations to come. Rights to the land—collective and individual, social and supernatural—are maintained by the interlocking and coordinate systems of Mossi social, political, and religious organization.

Land falls under one of four categories. First there is land used for the household settlements and the farms. It is held by the living members of the patrilineage in trust for the ancestral spirits and future generations; most rights to use are individual within the agnatic group. Second there is public land, that used for pathways and marketplaces. It is under the authority of the village chief, the living representative of the spirits of former village chiefs and the local representative of the king, who is endowed with authority by his own royal ancestors who have enjoined him to hold the land in trust for future kings and their subjects. Third there are the sacred places on the land, the Earth shrines. These are controlled by the Earth priest. Control of the "bush," unoccupied land that lies beyond the farms, is also shared by the village chief and the Earth priest.

The first category, land held by the Mossi agnatic descent group, is most important in the economic system. Final temporal authority over farmlands that belong to the kin group rests with the sib headman, *ni kiema,* whose authority is sanctioned by the ancestral spirits. It was they who first cleared and cultivated the land and established the system for its proper tenure. They left it for their descendants and continue to watch over it for them. The sib headman must see that this trust is not violated, that the system established by the ancestors for allocating and working the land is perpetuated.

In practice the responsibility for supervising land allocation and use is assumed by the elders, *sak kasemse,* of the component lineages of the sib, each of whom is the head of a separate residential kin group, or patriclan, which functions economically as a semi-autonomous unit. Sib and patriclan elders are immediately responsible for assuring that all able-bodied, mature male members of the lineage have access to proprietorship over farmlands adequate to provide for the subsistence needs of themselves and their dependents. It is the elders who must see that these lands are allocated and worked in the traditionally correct way, according to the ancestors' will.

Rights of individual proprietorship over specific fields are determined by patrilineal descent within the elementary family. When a man dies, control of his fields is passed to his eldest son who must see that his father's co-wives and all his younger sons have land

enough to work. This is difficult. For the constantly shifting, irregu-
larly demarcated farmlands of the Mossi cannot be easily divided.
Inequalities are inevitable and they grow in seriousness as the
deceased man's sons mature and their own elementary families
multiply. To avoid conflict, the Mossi believe that a man's sons
should try to work communally the fields they have inherited from
him. These are, of course, in addition to the rights of individual
proprietorship to other fields they have already received from him
and from other senior members of the lineage prior to his death. As
each son's own elementary family grows, this cooperative endeavor
becomes increasingly difficult to sustain. As (1) the eldest brother's
concern for the welfare of his own dependents, for example, takes
priority over his interest in preserving his younger brother's rights,
as (2) land is reallocated in the process of crop rotation and fallowing, as (3) the size of the patriclan increases, and as (4) the process
of erosion and soil debilitation progresses, the potential for conflict
mounts steadily and disputes arise. The task of the lineage elder in
arbitrating conflict between fellow clansmen becomes increasingly
difficult. From time to time, despite everyone's good intentions,
things get to the point where there just is not sufficient land to provide all members of the patriclan with enough to make a living.

Some of the members of the kin group must leave, to resolve
their problem in one of several ways. Very young men can seek
work temporarily as laborers in the cities of the Sudanic region or
in Ghana or the Ivory Coast and may remain away until land is
available for them at home, usually when their younger male siblings
have matured sufficiently to go off as migrant workers themselves
and some of their sisters have married, thus decreasing their fathers'
need to retain their own extensive holdings. Or young men in need
of land may ask for permission to live and work with their mothers'
patrilineage, a request always granted if land is available. Some
without sufficient fields may request the permission of the village
chief and the Earth priest to clear and cultivate unused land in the
bush. But in many instances the Mossi must leave their communities
and seek land in other villages. In either of these two latter
instances settlement some distance from the farmlands of the
patriclan marks the first stage in the process of lineage fission.

If a conflict over land occurs within the lineage and cannot be
resolved by the lineage elder, or if disputes arise within the com-

ponent lineages of the sib, the case is referred to the sib headman. If he cannot settle it, and it is not resolved by the departure of one of the disputants, the conflict may ultimately be taken to the village chief, the final local source of legal authority. The chief makes his decision after consultation with the council of village elders, which is comprised of the headmen of all the localized descent groups.

Thus control over farmland rests most immediately, but least importantly, with the individual proprietor, then with the extended family head, the lineage elder, the sib headman, and finally with the village chief and his counselors. In theory a dispute over land might be carried beyond the village chief to the canton chief, to the provincial chief, and finally, but only theoretically, to the Yatenga Naba himself. In practice, disputes within the sib are usually settled there. Generally only conflicts over land between unrelated kin groups are taken to the chiefs.

Each Mossi farmer has authority to decide the uses to which land under his proprietorship will be put. He determines which fields will be planted to what crops and which will be left fallow. The allocation of fields for the cultivation of particular crops must, of course, be made on the basis of both technological and economic criteria. Given the quality of the soil and the supply of workers available, the farmer must decide which of the several staple crops can be most efficiently produced.

However, because of the shortage of land in Yatenga, need and the right to use are necessarily linked. If a man has the right to proprietorship over more land than he can cultivate effectively, any of his male agnates in need can ask and expect to receive permission to use a portion of his holding, either for themselves or for their wives and children. Such a request is usually made to the proprietor of the field himself. If he is uncooperative, the lineage elder may be asked to intercede. However every Mossi understands that it is the will of the ancestors that the land be used in the best interest of the lineage as a collectivity. To violate the ancestors' will is to risk serious punishment. Consequently, clearly justified requests for the reallocation of fields are usually granted readily, if not without some resentment. If the reason a farmer is not using all his fields is temporary—due to the illness or absence of some of his sons, for example—such reallocation takes the form of a loan and is witnessed by the elders of the lineage.

In such cases the borrower is usually required to allow the former proprietor continued and exclusive rights to gather the firewood and the fruits and leaves of the shrubs and trees growing on the land. For in both the inheritance and borrowing of land, claims on the use of perrenial plants and trees are transmitted or retained independently of shifts in the right to land use itself. The person who borrows a field must, of course, agree not to lend it to another. If these conditions are not observed, the land can be reclaimed by its original proprietor at any time. At the harvest the new user of a borrowed field may occasionally make a present of grain to the former proprietor. When such a loan is made within the lineage or patriclan, a gift is unnecessary.

The loan of farmland to a nonmember of the descent group must have the consent of the lineage or sib elder. Usually this is given only if the prospective borrower is affinally related to the lineage or is the bond-friend of the lender. In the instance of a loan made outside the lineage, the gift made by the borrower after each harvest is important not only for its compensatory value but as a means of reaffirming annually the original proprietor's claim. So long as this limitation is observed and relations remain friendly, and so long as the proprietor's kinsmen do not press him for the use of the field, the arrangement can be perpetuated for years and can even be inherited by the borrower's son. But he must, as did his father, recognize the status of the rightful proprietor with an annual gift.

Every Mossi must have farmland in order to live. The quality of the soils, their relative fertility and potential productivity, vary each season. And the size and composition of the farmers' families are constantly varying also. Births, marriages, illnesses, absences, and deaths create constant shifts in the subsistence needs of each farmer and his dependents. The Mossi system of land allocation reflects this; the alternatives are as important as the rules. To maintain balance in the relations between men and the land, flexibility is perhaps the single condition most important for assuring socioeconomic stability and continuity.

Women do not inherit the right to use land. It is the duty of their husbands to provide them with sufficient fields. A woman can also request land from her husband's brothers or from his father. When she dies or is divorced, the fields she has worked are usually taken over by her sons or her husband's brothers. If she remains with her husband's patriclan after his death, either marrying his brother or attaching herself to the household of a married son, she is usually permitted to retain the right to the fields she needs to support herself. Women can also lend their fields. Most often the borrower is an adolescent son, a friendly co-wife, or a son's wife. But such a loan can only be made with the permission of the field's original proprietor.

At the level of each component unit in the residential kin group—the nuclear family, the polygynous family, the extended family, and in the patriclan itself—certain of the fields held individually by the headman of each unit are worked communally by all members of that unit. Thus, for example, in the extended family the father has final authority over the allocation of all farmland used by his wives and children. Certain fields are under the more specific proprietorship of each of his mature sons who may in turn delegate the right to use them to their wives and their own sons. In each instance such fields are worked principally by their respective specific proprietors who have the first right to their products. However most of the fields held by the head of the extended family are worked with the help of his wife or his wives and children, by any younger brothers who might be attached to his household, and, occasionally, by a sister's son who has come to reside with his mother's brother.

The produce from these fields is stored in the granaries of the family head. There it is drawn upon principally to meet the individual needs of his household: to feed his wives and dependent children, to pay his tax, to be used as part of the bridewealth payment made by his sons when they marry, to offer hospitality to visitors, and to provide for the preparation of the millet gruel and millet beer used in sacrifical libations. But the millet in the granaries of the family head serves also as an emergency store to be used by any member of the family in need. This pattern of organization, on a smaller or larger scale—with more or less fields worked communally depending on the size and needs of the particular family group—structures economic relations in each component unit of the patriclan.

These individually held, but communally worked fields are called "lineage land," *boodooziedo*. The fields held by the sib headman have the same status, but usually communal rights to the products from them are only of economic significance to the localized membership of the sib, especially the members of the sib headman's own patriclan. The inheritance rule for such communal land—whether it is held by the head of the elementary family, the extended family, the lineage elder, or the sib headman—differs from the rule that applies to fields worked individually. The holding is not passed on to the eldest son of the deceased but is transmitted to his eldest surviving brother when he succeeds to the status of headman.

Thus inheritance and borrowing are the two principal means by which land and residential sites are acquired among the Mossi. Both processes generally function with adequate flexibility to provide for the necessary adjustment of land rights to the changing needs of the farmer and his kinsmen. The occasional failure of the system to provide adequately for the land requirements of some members of a quickly growing patriclan is dealt with through the activation of the variety of alternative patterns of work and residence just described: labor migration, affiliation with mother's patrilineage, the fission of a lineage segment, or, infrequently, the total dissolution of kinship ties and the establishment of an economically, socially, and ritually independent unit which ultimately becomes the founding lineage of a new sib.

Most other productive goods among the Mossi are held in accordance with these same two overlapping categories of corporate and individual proprietary rights. Both categories limit use and reallocation ; neither permits permanent disposal. No individual and no group has the right to alienate land. This is true of most other productive goods among the Mossi as well.

The grinding platforms and sun shelters used by the entire patriclan are also held by the lineage as a corporate entity. The elder of the lineage is charged with overseeing their maintenance and arbitrates disputes over rights to equal use. These goods are, of course, not inherited. They are never disposed of but are only abandoned—because they are no longer in condition to be used, because the size of the patriclan has decreased and they are no longer needed, or because the kin group residence is moved.

Rights to the use of houses and granaries are transmitted

patrileneally on a generational basis and are held temporarily by a succession of individual proprietors. Thus the house and granaries of an elementary family head, patriclan elder, or sib headman are passed on at his death to his senior surviving brother. This may occasion a shift in the proprietary rights of all male agnates in the minimal lineage involved. It may also precipitate an intragenerational shift in property rights, for when a man's brother inherits the house and granaries of his elder sibling, his own house passes on to his brother's elder son. His brother's younger son inherits from his elder sibling and so on. In practice, of course, every death in the lineage does not have this domino-like effect. Most Mossi houses and granaries are much alike, and shifting residence within the patriclan is rarely worth the trouble. It is usually only the successor to a position of headmanship within one of the component units of the patriclan who actually moves his household.

Like the right to use farmland, rights to the use of houses or granaries can be granted to any close agnatic kinsman in need. Such rights are also freely extended to sisters' sons. As with fields lent to the son of a daughter of the lineage, the rights to the use of such houses and granaries can be passed on to sister's son's son in accordance with the usual rule of patrilineal inheritance.

The inherited right to the individual proprietorship of productive goods other than land is also always limited by need. A man who inherits the use of a house or granaries he does not need is morally obligated to initiate their reallocation. Because he cannot use them for production and because they are not a negotiable form of wealth, it is to his advantage to do so. His economic interest is best served not by keeping them, but by accumulating good will in redistributing them.

Handtools such as hoes and knives are the only productive goods privately owned by the Mossi. These are purchased from the smiths and then transmitted by inheritance within the extended family. But even the tools a farmer purchases in the market must be lent to any kinsman in need. Tools once acquired are rarely resold, but are occasionally given as gifts. They are the only productive goods of which a Mossi farmer can permanently dispose.

THE ORGANIZATION OF WORK

The Kinship Basis

With the exception of the manufacture of certain tools all work importantly connected with the basic subsistence technology of the Mossi is organized according to a pattern determined first by the kinship system and then by sex and age.[1] Outside the kinship system, differences in economic and social status play only a secondary role in the organization of work. Expectably, the system for allocating responsibility for directing the performance of the various tasks involved in farm work follows the patterned allocation of rights to land use.

Just as the head of each family group in the patriclan is responsible for allocating farmland to his wives and children, so is he charged with regulating and coordinating their work. His status as head of the family sanctions his authority in deciding which crops are to be planted in which fields, which fields are to be left fallow, and when each of the many activities connected with cultivation is to be taken up. He has the right to appropriate the services and direct the work of his dependents, his wives and children, and he may also request the assistance of any other of his younger siblings. Occasionally he may also seek the aid of his bond-friend or another of his associates. Which of these several relationships is activated and to what extent depends on his needs and his means of meeting them, circumstances that vary throughout the season and from year to year. Variation in the organization of work is the constant among the Mossi, for adaptability to shifting environmental, technological, and social conditions is always essential to economic survival.

Sex and Age and The Organization of Work

Sex, modified by considerations of age, complements status in the kin group as a determinant in the organization of work. Usually

1. The organization of the data that follow owes much to the important analysis made by Stanley H. Udy, Jr. (*The Organization of Work,* New Haven: RAF Press, 1959 and "Preindustrial Forms of Organized Work," in W. E. Moore and A. S. Feldman (eds.), *Labor Commitment and Social Change in Developing Areas,* New York: Social Science Research Council, pp. 78–91), 1960.

it is men between fifteen and forty-five who undertake the heavier tasks associated with farm work, such as the clearing and cleaning of the fields. However even at this they are frequently assisted by their wives and young children who follow them breaking up the clods and collecting dry brush for burning. Women and children also assist in collecting fertilizer for the field. And adults of both sexes work at planting, cultivation, and the harvest.

Only women who are menstruating, and thus regarded as ritually unclean, abstain from work on the farms. Otherwise a woman's responsibility for participating in all but the heaviest aspects of farm work is lightened only when she is in the advanced stages of pregnancy or has just borne a child. At harvest time women follow their husbands through the field collecting the heads of millet grain from the stalk. They help dry the grain and assist in transporting it back to the settlement for storage. Gleaning of the fields after the harvest and collecting dried millet stalks to be used for firewood and forage are essentially women's tasks. They are almost always assisted by their unmarried daughters and by their sons so long as they are too small to work with their fathers.

In addition to the responsibility of assisting their husbands with all aspects of field work, women and all boys old enough to have been allocated land take individual initiative in working fields of their own. While the head of the elementary family is formally responsible for the proper conduct of this work, he rarely finds it necessary to interfere. Women have the right to request the help of their husbands, especially with the heavier tasks of clearing and cleaning the fields before planting. A woman can also appropriate the help of any of her children before and after they marry. But with daughters who marry outside the local community this is, of course, difficult. Women also have the right to assistance from their daughters-in-law, and sometimes they are helped by their younger unmarried sisters. Co-wives assist one another on a voluntary basis, but only if they are friendly. With marriage a woman's ties to her bond-friends and age mates—always looser than those of a man to his associates—are weakened still further by her responsibility to her husband's patriclan, and often by distance as well. Consequently women can rarely rely for assistance on their associates outside the kinship system.

"A woman's responsibility for participating in all but the heaviest aspects of field work is lightened only when she is in the advanced stages of pregnancy or has just borne a child."

In addition to their work on the farms, Mossi women are responsible for the processing and preservation of all food. Meat, which is butchered by men, is the only exception. In polygamous households co-wives alternate in preparing their husbands meals. Or, as has been noted, if they cooperate easily they may work together in the preparation of several dishes which they serve to him and also share among themselves.

A woman's duties also include gathering the leaves and fruit of the many wild plants used in cooking. And it is women who prepare millet beer and the other beverages the Mossi consume. They also draw and carry the water used in cooking and washing and for household baths. With the assistance of their children they gather firewood and forage. They care for the clothing belonging to their husbands and children and are responsible for their husband's houses and keeping their courtyards freshly swept.

Husbands and wives rarely assist one another in garden work. It is an individual endeavor undertaken for money profit. Often as much as half of a gardener's produce is sold in the market or used to make personal gifts. If a man were to solicit his wife's assistance in his garden or if she were to ask him for help, this would create an obligation to share in the distribution of the produce. Further, the Mossi say a man should avoid asking for his wife's help with garden work because a portion of the garden produce is usually sold for money. Because cash is frequently used by men to make gifts to other women in return for their sexual favors, it is feared a jealous wife might use her husband's obligation to her to justify publicly berating him and the women to whom he had made such gifts. Thus gardening is as private as any Mossi economic enterprise can be.

Because land for gardens comes from the patriclan, a portion of the produce must be contributed to the sustenance of the kin group, usually the members of the gardener's elementary family. But the remainder can be sold and the profits need not be shared. The right to private profit is legitimate only so long as work is not shared. When men and women require help with their gardens, they usually turn to their children or to younger siblings whom they pay with a part of the money they earn in the market.

It is, of course, the responsibility of the women to care for their children. And it is they who assume the principal role in educating

"Among the very young, the sex-based division of labor is considerably weaker."

their daughters and preparing them for marriage. They are also expected to prepare food for their husband's visitors and friends and to care for their husband's mothers—to clean their houses and make their meals when they are too old to manage these tasks for themselves. In return men cut firewood for their wives and leave it in the bush for them to collect. Sometimes a man agrees to weave his wife's thread into cotton bands which she then gives to him or another male kinsman to sell. Usually the arrangement is reciprocal. The woman spins her husband's cotton into thread in return for the weaving he does for her.

In the past the male roles of warrior and hunter complemented the exclusively female tasks associated with housekeeping. This, of course, can no longer be so. To an extent, migratory labor has taken the place of going off to war. At least it is an almost entirely masculine endeavor.

The traditionally special role of more mature Mossi men has been preserved: They are still leaders in the political and religious activities of their kin group and communities. Here, as in farm work, their responsibilities are largely ascribed by their status in the kinship system, modified slightly by considerations of age, health, and ability.

Among the very young, the sex-based division of labor is considerably weaker. The tasks assigned small children are much the same regardless of their sex. Little boys often help their mothers and sisters with the gathering of firewood or wild plants, and young girls frequently accompany their brothers in herding sheep and goats. The first tasks assigned children in the fields are also much the same: carrying water and food, helping with the collection of brush for burning, and breaking up the clods of newly turned earth.

Although the first separation of boys' and girls' activities occurs for reasons that are superficially social, it results in their beginning to learn the differing tasks that will be their adult responsibilities. As soon as a boy is old enough to feed himself, he is sent to eat with his father and the other men of the lineage, and from that time on he is encouraged to remain with them when not performing some specific task for his mother. Although a very small girl is sometimes taken by her father or grandfather to join the men at mealtime, and is fed upon his lap, this lasts for only a short time. Soon she begins to take her meals regularly with her mother and sisters.

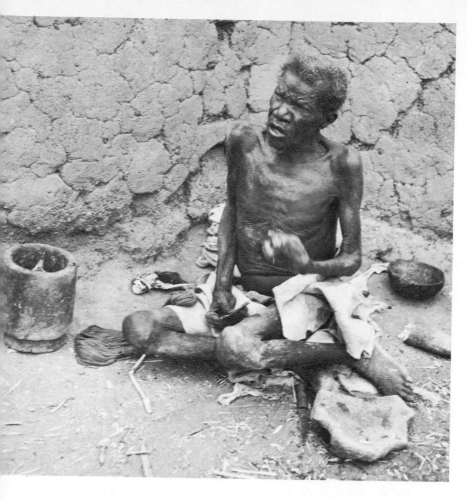

". . . those too feeble to work in the fields remain in the patriclan residence."

Boys begin early to run errands for their elder male kinsmen.
They sit beside the old men as they repair tools, they are given
greater responsibility than their sisters in the herding of animals,
and well before adolescence they have begun to help in the millet
fields, gradually assuming the more arduous aspects of the work of
cleaning, planting, hoeing, weeding, and harvesting. By early
adolescence a boy has learned all of the techniques of farm work
and will shortly be assigned his own field.

The small girls who remain to eat with their mothers and the
other adult women of the patriclan soon begin to help with cooking
as well as gathering firewood and wild foods. They are sent to the
wells for water, assume part of the responsibility for the care of
their younger brothers and sisters, and are given cotton to spin into
thread. With their brothers they join their parents in farm work at
the age of seven or eight. By the beginning of puberty, girls have
acquired all the skills expected of a Mossi wife and mother, a role
they usually assume at thirteen or fourteen, two or three years after
the onset of puberty.

Among the aged those too feeble to work in the fields remain in
the patriclan residence. If they are able, the old men repair tools
and weave mats. Old women tend the children and the kitchen fires.
In the rainy months, when all able-bodied members of the patriclan
are often away in the fields from dawn until early dark, the old
people guard the settlements from thieves and watch over any young
children left behind. As with small children, men and women of
greatly advanced age are treated much alike in the assignment of
tasks; a very elderly man may sometimes be left to tend the kitchen
fire of his son's wife or assigned some other task generally performed only by a woman. And old women, especially those who
have returned to their natal patriclans to live out their last years,
often sit with the old men of their families, assist them with their
simple tasks, and consult with them on the conduct of lineage
affairs.

So long as they can function physically and socially, the old
among the Mossi are valued for their accumulated wisdom and for
their knowledge of traditional lore. Advanced age brings high status
to the senior members of the lineage. Although they retain formal
authority so long as they remain mentally alert, there is a tendency
for their more youthful future successors to usurp the direction of

affairs in the kin group. Those who are senile are treated, not unkindly, but with casual disregard. The Mossi fear this. The abandonment of work in the fields is symbolic of the onset of senility that means not only the loss of physical powers but an eventual decline in status and authority as well. Frequently old men resist giving up their accustomed tasks and defy their younger kinsmens' encouragement to relax their work load. Old women do not risk the same loss of status and authority because their position is subordinate from the outset and because, once they have passed the age of childbearing, their social position becomes somewhat analogous to that of their male fellow elders.

In every aspect of the organization of work within the patriclan the individual economic activity and personal economic interest of every member is subordinated to the interests of his elders and to the kin group as a corporate entity. From the time in early childhood when a Mossi learns the first simple tasks that mark the beginning of his economic cooperation with his kinsmen, he is taught that not he alone but the entire group will suffer if he fails to perform well the tasks assigned to him. If, for example, he allows one of the animals he is tending to stray, he will suffer punishment from its owner, as well as his father, and will also earn the stern disapproval of all his kinsmen who hear what he has done. Any elder kinsman can send him on an errand to another household, entrust him with a younger child to watch, or call for his assistance in drawing water at the well or gathering firewood.

He soon learns also that any older relative can punish him instantly and severely if he does not do what is defined as his share of the work, or if he does it badly. As his elders gradually retire from participation in the more arduous and important productive tasks, his own work, affecting the material well-being of the entire kin group, will increase in importance. This explains his elders' stern attention to his performance of the tasks assigned him as a child and a youth.

Everything a Mossi receives during the most formative years of his life, from birth to late adolescence, comes from his kinsmen with the understanding that it is his right because he is their obedient and dutiful son. As he matures, this lesson is reinforced. Without his kinsmen he could not participate in the traditional technology and economy. He could neither acquire farmland nor receive the assistance needed to work it. And without land he could not establish a family. Separated from the lineage and patriclan, his legal identity would be blurred and his political rights lost. For his relations with his kin group, especially with his elders, provide the only legitimate channel for political expression and the achievement of political status.

Without his kinsmen he is equally cut off from any means of maintaining security in relation to the supernatural, for a disobedient son risks both the curse of the ancestral spirits and the loss of any means of achieving expiation. Without land he is also without a means of maintaining contact with the Earth deity.

Reliance on the kin group and the necessity of economic self-subordination, the first things a Mossi learns as a child, are thus profoundly reinforced as his experience of the workings of his culture grows.

Members of the several units within the patriclan also cooperate in nonagricultural work. As usual the pressure for such mutual aid is strongest among the male agnates within the extended family. Although animals are owned by adults of both sexes on an indivdual basis, they are usually tended communally by the children of the component family units of the patriclan. Kinsmen also assist one another in the repair and maintenance of their houses and household goods. Compensation for such assistance takes the valuable form of a perpetuated obligation to reciprocate.

Work and Rank

Differences in rank are of even less significance than differences in sex and age in the organization of work among the Mossi. Certain social, political, and religious positions—usually combined with advanced age—occasionally result in differences in work organization. But only a few individuals are affected. Thus, for example, the sib headman may sometimes be so occupied with the responsibilities related to the administration of family or community affairs that a portion of what would otherwise be his share of the farm work is taken over by his younger kinsmen. Occasionally a village chief may be kept from work in the fields for the same reason. Such important figures can usually be confident of the assistance of their kinsmen,

who willingly work for them in return for the advantage of maintaining a relationship of potentially useful mutual obligation with
important persons. Although the Earth priests must also devote a
part of their time to sacerdotal duties, most of the rituals at which
they officiate occur during the dry season and thus do not interfere
with their work as farmers.

In fact all rituals, both religious and political, are so organized
that farm work is rarely interfered with. The Mossi ceremonial
cycle only gets underway after the harvests, when the grain is in the
storehouses and the hardest work of the year is over.

The Diffuseness of Tasks

It would be an exaggeration to say that specialized tasks are
totally deferred to the dry season. Even during the rainy months
few jobs require the undivided attention of the worker, except for
short periods during planting, cultivation, and the harvest. Otherwise in a single day a farmer may weed a part of his field or garden,
see to the minor repair of a tool, patch the roof of his granary,
arrange for the sale of some cotton bands, cut some firewood for
his wife, and visit his bond-friend to discuss a projected joint
commercial enterprise. This diffuseness is, of course, even more
characteristic of the work schedule of a woman, who must com-
bine and coordinate such household tasks as cooking, cleaning,
gathering firewood, and tending her children with work in her husband's fields and in her own garden. She is also a part-time trader
and a food gatherer. Any or all of these activities may be performed during a single day. Some of them, such as household tasks
and child care or gathering firewood and wild food, are performed
simultaneously.

The Custodial Basis of Work Organization

Coercion was probably never a very important basis for work
organization among the Mossi; certainly it is not now. And there is
little reason to assume it ever could have been. Mossi technology is
too unproductive to allow for the profitable exploitation of the work
of others. Before the European conquest of Yatenga the Mossi had
slaves. The power of the masters was unlimited in theory, and there

was a tendency to assign slaves the more onerous tasks, but there did not exist, as there does not exist today, the technological basis necessary for the development of markedly significant differences in work based on differences in status. Then as now everybody, master and slave, had to farm in order to eat. But now the slaves have all been emancipated.[2]

Today the only significantly distinctive work organized on a basis that might be referred to as custodial is that of the smiths, members of descent groups regarded as being indigenous to Yatenga. As a group the smiths are endogamous. The right to perform their special work is ascribed on the basis of their separate social identity, and a distinctive ritual aura is ascribed both to their work and to them as persons. In these several ways, but only in these ways, the Mossi smiths constitute a caste.[3] Metalworking and pottery making are their exclusive prerogatives. Most carpenters are also smiths.

However, for the smiths, as for other Mossi, craft specialization is primarily a dry-season occupation. During the rainy months they accept tools for emergency repairs but do not otherwise work at their trade. They are too busy in the fields. With the smiths also it is the kinship system that determines the basic organization of work on the farms, in the mines, and at the forge and the kiln. The right to the use of farmland and the organization of workers follows the pattern already described.[4] The usual productive unit is comprised of the male members of an extended family. Seniority assures the right to assume initiative, but personal inclination is also important. Thus, while all the Mossi, including the smiths, participate fully in farm work, not all members of the descent groups of the smiths work with metal, pottery, and wood. Those who enjoy the work and are good at it take the lead. Others mildly interested and moderately proficient assist them. And some others have nothing to do with metalworking and pottery making at all.

2.   For mention of the political status of the descendants of slaves see Chapter 6, p. 155.

3.   Otherwise social groups in Mossi society are not ranked hierarchically or separated by significant differences in socioeconomic position or ritual status.

4.   The land from which iron ore is taken for smelting and the area from which clay is collected are held by smith sibs and worked by members of their component patriclans.

Just as the smiths confine their specialized economic activities largely to the dry season, so do other Mossi specialists—those who spend part of their time during the dry months working at house construction, at the manufacture of baskets and mats, as weavers, or as traders. But once the rains begin, such activities are abandoned or much reduced and fitted into the routine organization of farm work made necessary by the weather and the growth of the crops. Neither the dry-season specialization of the smiths based on a difference in the social status of the group nor the special work based on individual proclivity or family tradition ever replace farming as the basic work of all the Mossi.

By an extension of the principle that identifies cooperation within the kin group as the most important means of maintaining individual security and collective well-being, the family-based work organization of the Mossi patriclans is occasionally made use of by the village chief. Workers are recruited by village sector. Because such sectors are usually comprised of the founding and component patriclans of a particular sib, this has the effect of mobilizing people already accustomed to working together and who share a common interest in maintaining an amicable relation with the village chief.

Usually only workers from a single sector are called at one time. When their services are needed, a formal announcement is made several evenings before, usually called out from the roof of the chief's residence or from high in the branches of a baobab tree growing in the sector of the village from which workers are to be recruited. The enforcement of compliance with this call to work is the duty of the elders of each patriclan. And it is they who direct their kinsmen in the performance of the tasks assigned. The Mossi say this work used to be compulsory. Now those who fail to cooperate are not punished. However it is the responsibility of the patriclan elders to maintain good relations between their kin groups and the chief, and their efforts to persuade their kinsmen to assist him are usually effective.

The Contractual Basis of Work Organization

Within the local community the most important contractual basis for work organization is formed by the combined membership of early adolescent male and female age sets. A typical work group is composed of about twenty young people. The leader of the boys' age set, assisted by the girls' leader contracts for and assumes direction of the work of the entire group. The organization is formed each year about the time of the first light rains when the Mossi farmers have begun to prepare for the growing season. Soon after the group is organized, their leaders volunteer their labor for a day in the fields belonging to the village chief. This initial endeavor serves to announce to the community that their services are available. After this other farmers in need of assistance contract with them for work. The leader and the farmer agree upon a cash price, which is determined by the size of the field and the task to be accomplished. The young people then set to work without supervision and are paid when the job is done. Because the work is performed collectively and the profits are shared equally by all participants, the laggard worker is quickly noticed and pressured by ridicule to do his share.

If there are no drummers among the members of the boys' age set, one is hired to accompany them at their work. The boys and girls form a line and move down through the field swinging their short hoes in unison and singing to the accompaniment of the drum. They usually work from dawn until midmorning and then stop to rest through the midday heat. Work is resumed early in the afternoon and usually completed before sundown. Then they are paid and go marching and singing home. The leader keeps the cash payments received until harvesttime when they are used to purchase millet cakes and beer at the festivals that follow. At this time some of the money is also often used to buy clothing for the work group members—head cloths and skirt material for the girls, shirts and caps for the boys.

The Mossi also work individually on a contractual basis. Such an arrangement usually involves the performance of specialized tasks such as brick making, house building, or weaving. But farm labor may also be contracted for. Such work is most often undertaken by men whose own past farming endeavors have been so curtailed by sickness, lack of assistance from their younger kinsmen, field blight, or the depradations of locusts that they cannot provide adequate food for their families and have nothing to sell in order to pay their taxes.

Toward the end of the growing season those with families suffering

". . . the boys and girls form a line and move down through the field swinging their short hoes in unison and singing to the accompaniment of drums."

from preharvest hunger or who are otherwise in need frequently offer to do farm work in return for an immediate payment in grain. Wages in money or goods are always contracted for ahead of time. Once an agreement has been reached, the worker usually sets his own schedule, laboring steadily or intermittently, depending on the nature of the task and the press of his own work, until the job is done. Several men, usually close agnatic kinsmen, sometimes sell their labor as a group, with their eldest member taking the initiative in negotiating the contract and directing their work. Young migrant laborers who go off to find employment in Ghana and the Ivory Coast also organize themselves in this way.[5]

For the Mossi farmers these several work groups provide a useful supplement to the regular labor force at critical points in the growing season. And for the Mossi youth they offer a productive and profitable means of affecting the transition between the status of children, when they have no fields of their own, and the time when boys go off as adolescents to work in Ghana, the Ivory Coast, and in cities elsewhere in the Western Sudan, and girls marry and are incorporated into the work organizations of their husbands' patriclans. For the Mossi economic system such work groups provide still another source of the flexibility necessary to sustain balance in the relationship between the people, their technology, and the land.

The Voluntary Basis of Work Organization

Tasks performed on a voluntary basis are most difficult to abstract from the systematically diffused organization of work among the Mossi. Yet it is self-interested cooperative endeavor. The assistance rendered to bond-friends, age mates, and neighbors is most frequently and usefully activated as an alternative to reliance on the organizations of work based on kinship or contract. Services voluntarily rendered both within and without the kinship system, with the expectation of reciprocity—sooner or later, in one form or another—provide Mossi work organization with a further useful source of structural flexibility. It goes on all the time. For example,

5. This organization has important implications for an assessment of the cultural effects of such contact with other people outside their homeland. Often it is only the senior member of a kin-based work group who comes into direct contact with non-Mossi employers.

on his way to his field a Mossi farmer may stop to help a neighbor repair the damaged roof of one of his granaries, or may join another in cultivating a field adjacent to his own, and on his way home in the evening he may help his elder brother's wife carry back the firewood she has gathered. Such casual voluntary work not only is productively important, but also serves as a significant means of maintaining the bonds of reciprocity that provide the Mossi individual and his community with an important source of economic and social security.

Although age-grade work groups and individual wage laborers are often employed by the Mossi, their utilization is always subsidiary. It never replaces reliance on the kin group as the principal source of workers. Because land is allocated on the basis of need, no man can keep much more than he needs to support his dependents. If he has dependents, they work and he doesn't need to hire laborers. Otherwise only chiefs or occasionally men more wealthy than their fellow Mossi can hire laborers. But even chiefs have difficulty in retaining the right to use more land than they need to support their households and to meet their responsibilities to redistribute their surplus in hospitality and in support of villagers in need.

DISTRIBUTION

The processes of redistribution, reciprocity, and market exchange all operate as aspects of the system by which the Mossi allocate the products of their work. However among these processes redistribution is most important in providing for the movement of the majority of goods and services basic to the satisfaction of the Mossi's material needs. Reciprocity is a process of only secondary significance. Traditionally market exchange has been a peripheral aspect of the Mossi economic system, but since the French colonial occupation it has come to be increasingly important as a mechanism for the movement of goods.

Redistribution

Land, the basic productive good in the Mossi economy, is allocated by means of a system that is essentially redistributive. Consumption goods, the products of work, move in the same manner.

Just as the head of each family unit within the patriclan has the right to allocate land among his dependents and to control their work, allocating or appropriating it in accordance with the needs of the patriclan as a productive unit, so does he have the right to allocate the product of his dependents' endeavors. However, in practice, each member of the family unit—father, mother, and male children old enough to work land of their own—all have the right to allocate the products taken from their own fields. These are stored in their respective granaries and used primarily to meet their own immediate needs. A woman is expected to use a part of her millet to feed herself and her young children. This is perceived as a return for the land given to her by her husband's kin group and for whatever assistance she has received from them with her farm work; she feeds their children in return. But the rest she can use as she wishes, selling it, giving it away, or storing it.

Similarly a man has the right to allocate the product from the fields under his immediate proprietorship. However, because his holdings are more extensive and his dependence on the assistance of his wives and children is greater, he must redistribute a larger portion of his harvest in accordance with their needs. They work his fields together. The product is stored in his granaries and distributed by him to each of his wives every few days. These granaries constitute the principal source of the family's food supply. If a surplus is produced in excess of the family's subsistence needs, and what is required for entertaining, for the tax, for seed, and for assisting the unmarried sons with marriage payments, it can be sold for cash.

The elementary family as a unit in the productive system functions nearly autonomously. Most of the product of its endeavors is redistributed among its own members. However, as was noted, most members of each elementary family are expected to work as well in the fields belonging to the elders of the extended family, the patriclan, and occasionally on the farmlands held by the sib headman as well. In turn the product from these fields is allocated to meet the needs of the entire kin group—to support the headman's household, to pay tribute to the village chief, to pay the tax, to entertain guests, to prepare the millet beer and gruel used in rituals, to assist younger members of the kin group in making marriage presents, and, perhaps most importantly, to provide a surplus to

". . . the product from these fields is allocated . . . to pay
tribute to the village chief . . ."

be redistributed by the elders to any member of the kin group in need.

Fields held by the sib headman are usually worked only by local members of its component lineages. And in practice it is only they who draw upon his stores. For members of the descent group whose patriclans are located in other villages, lands held by the sib headman are only a symbolic source of economic security.

The process for the allocation of goods within the patriclan and its component units is paralleled by the manner in which the villagers sustain the political system. The crops harvested on the chief's farmlands with the assistance of the villagers are similarly redistributed. A part goes for the maintenance of his household, for the tax, for the entertainment of visitors, for the preparation of sacrificial libations of millet gruel and beer, and for tribute to the canton and provincial chiefs and the king. A final part is retained in his storehouses to be redistributed to villagers in need.

Just as with the allocation of land and labor, the right of superiors in either the kinship system or the political system to appropriate and reallocate farm produce is sanctioned by their status in the authority system and reinforced by the power of the ancestral spirits. But they retain this right and the material support that makes it meaningful only so long as they remain responsive to the needs of their subordinates. If they fail to do so, they risk both the withdrawal of their support and the possibility of supernatural punishment.

A redistributive system is one of mutual dependence. It is only stable so long as the needs of at least most of the participants are met most of the time. The elementary and extended family heads, the patriclan elder, the sib headman, the village chief, canton chief, provincial chief, and the king must all have the support of their subordinates to maintain their status. If their dependents defect, and the Mossi social system is full of alternative sources of social and economic security, they are lost. Tradition sanctions their rights to appropriation and reallocation only so long as redistribution is equitable. A man who fails to give his wives their fair share of millet will be divorced. If he does not assist his sons with their marriage presents, they may take up residence with their mothers' brothers. An extended family head who is not generous in meeting the needs of his younger brothers or married sons knows that he may be deserted and left to work his land alone. A patriclan elder guilty of an analogous lapse would risk deposition, a chief, removal from office, the king, revolt and the punishment of his ancestors.

Thus most productive goods and most consumption goods move by means of a process that is essentially redistributive. Reciprocity and market exchange—the temporary loan of a field or the sale of labor for wages—are processes of secondary importance which provide useful flexibility to the economic system but are relatively less vital to its functioning. However they must also be considered. For an understanding of the workings of both reciprocity and the market are necessary for a full comprehension of the organization of the Mossi economy. And each of these processes is likely to increase in importance as the economy comes to be more affected by external forces.

Reciprocity

Within and between the component units of the patriclan some subsistence goods, principally food and clothing, move by a process that can best be described as reciprocal, although it does not meet all the criteria contained in Polanyi's classic definition of such a system. It does not, for example, "involve the movement of goods between correlative points of symmetrical groupings."[6] It is simpler than that. If one farmer in the patriclan gives grain to another who is short, the other is expected, sooner or later, to reciprocate, but not necessarily in kind. When a Mossi man gives several bundles of millet to his younger brother whose harvests were damaged by an invasion of migratory locusts, he does not expect and perhaps will not receive a return gift of an equal amount of grain. But he has a right to expect and will receive something, or some things, of approximately equal value—a goat, help in repairing the roof of his granary, perhaps over a period of several months a variety of

6. The classic definition for this type of system has been provided by Polanyi in a work he edited with C. W. Arensberg and H. W. Pearson (*Trade and Markets in the Early Empires,* Chicago: The Free Press, 1957). However the basic heuristic value of the model is not affected by the fact that certain types of reciprocity, as among the Mossi, lack the structural symmetry ascribed by Polanyi to the organization of this relation.

small presents in the form of goods and services which add up to an equivalent value—two or three cigarettes when he sees him in the market, a kola nut when he passes his field, a calabash of millet beer in the evening, a tin of powdered coffee brought back from Ghana, the use of his burro for a trip to the capital, an egg for his wife, and the loan of his dark glasses. In practice, before he has received an equal amount in return, he may ask his younger brother for some maize, which at this point in their protracted transactions reverses the obligation. Then the next gift should move the other way.

All the Mossi, men, women, and children, participate in this system and are usually involved in several such reciprocal relations at any time. For the individual the perpetuation of as many mutual obligations as possible serves simply as an efficient means of extending the sources of his social security. The object is not to close such transactions, but to keep them going.

Control in this system of exchange is affected in two ways. First, gifts of considerable worth are almost always made in the presence of others. This makes public the fact and the extent of the receiver's obligation. Second, a persistent failure to reciprocate adequately will cause gossip to be purposefully started by the dissatisfied partner to the exchange relation. Shame and the pressure exerted by the kinsmen of the laggard participant, who are fearful for the good name and credit standing of their lineage, will usually do the rest. Perhaps of equal importance, the person who fails to reciprocate generously will soon be known and will find it difficult to establish this valued relation with others. Reciprocal relations of this sort are constantly forming and reforming within kin groups and between individuals and groups otherwise unrelated. As a matter of fact, reciprocity is the most important process for the exchange of goods outside the kinship system. It is only the near autonomy of the patriclan as the source of its members' subsistence needs that makes reciprocity a process of secondary importance in the operation of the Mossi economy.

The relationship of the Mossi to the Fulani herdsmen of Yatenga manifests particularly well the ambivalence characteristic of many of their reciprocal economic arrangements. Each group—Mossi and Fulani—profits from the exchange and values its perpetuation, yet each fears that the other may be taking advantage secretly, abusing his rights to the detriment of the other. The Mossi farmers regard their Fulani partners with great distrust. They contend that the herdsmen who take their cattle north out of Yatenga during the growing season never lose their own beasts, but that it is only the animals belonging to the Mossi that go astray, are stolen, fall sick, or prove to be barren. Again the public exchange of goods and services between the two groups is the principal means of ensuring mutual compliance with the rules of the relationship. The Mossi farmers also joke with their Fulani partners, and, as always, such levity provides a measure of control by allowing for the concomitant maintenance of communication and the discharge of hostile sentiments in a culturally permissible way. This attitude of exasperated distrust reinforces the social distance and cultural distinctiveness that separate the Mossi from the Fulani, despite their interdependence.

Market Exchange

Traditionally Mossi markets are held every third day in an open area between village sectors. Commerce in differing varieties of merchandise is roughly segregated by area. Today there are probably more than one hundred markets in Yatenga. Prior to the European conquests there were said to have been only six.[7,8] As the figure suggests, market exchange plays only a tertiary role in the allocation of basic subsistence goods among the Mossi. Land does not enter the market at all; and for the most part labor is only available for sale after subsistence work has been accomplished. Traditionally only surplus or luxury goods moved through the market.

The market has limited, but not unimportant functions. First it allows for the distribution of farm and garden surpluses both within the local community and between communities. However because environmental conditions are relatively uniform throughout Yatenga, since climatic variations are slight, and because there is no technological specialization from region to region, this economic role is of limited significance, allowing only for the adjustment of

7. Zahan (1954, p. 373).
8. For a description of a Mossi market see Skinner (1962).

necessarily slight differences in the availability of some subsistence commodities.

Second the marketplace is important as a center for the maintenance of redistributive and reciprocal ties. For example, an encounter at the market with a distant agnatic kinsman often results in the activation of the relation as a means of obtaining assistance with farm work. Or a farmer residing with his mother's patriclan may be reminded by a meeting with the elder of his own descent group that a presentation of grain should be made to compensate for his failure to work in the latter's fields. A market encounter with his wife's father may provide a man with the opportunity to give him a calabash of beer as a part of the on-going system of bridewealth payments. As an investment in continued good relations with his in-laws or bond-friends, he may use a meeting in the market to cement their reciprocal tie with an exchange of kola nuts and an agreement to work together the coming week in one another's fields.

The function of the Mossi market thus appears to be essentially adjustive. It provides for the reallocation of surplus subsistence goods remaining after redistributive and reciprocal responsibilities have been met and, as the principal setting for the encounter of Mossi farmers who are otherwise largely taken up with the affairs of their respective semiautonomous patriclan settlements, it provides indirectly for the activation and perpetuation of such redistributive and reciprocal ties.

The market is also important because it provides for the exchange of goods peripheral to subsistence. Most goods produced by the individual as a private entrepreneur move through the market. Given the amount of leisure available to the Mossi, the fact that such goods are not more abundant—a factor that sharply limits the economic significance of the Mossi market—requires some explanation.

A Mossi only has the clear right to dispose privately of what he has produced if he has employed only productive goods belonging to himself and if he has used only his own labor. In fact these conditions can never be entirely met. Land, for example, is an essential element in the production of almost any consumption good among the Mossi. And land is never privately owned. Nor does a Mossi "own" his own labor so exclusively that he can employ it as he wishes without incurring obligations to his kinsmen. His

"The market is also important as it provides for the exchange of goods peripheral to subsistence."

economic ties to his kin group are too diffuse to allow for that. If, for example, a man has been granted the right to proprietorship over a field and decides, after making his contribution to the material support of the kin group in other ways, that he wants to use this particular field to grow cotton for cash, his rights to dispose of his crop are affected by the fact that the land belongs to the lineage. Thus he could not deny the request of a kinsman for a loan of part of the money he receives without risking severe criticism and the possibility of future economic retaliation when he, in turn, might be in need of assistance. In other words, individual proprietary rights to land, the only condition under which land can be held, does not imply an exclusively private right to dispose of the product taken from it. All the farmer has is the right to initiate the process of disposal. But the proper pattern for this process is determined by a tradition that requires sharing. This is a circumstance that affects the Mossi market and market behavior importantly.

For the diffuse claims on what is likely in any case to be a small profit discourage extensive reliance on entrepreneurship as a means of getting a living, much less "getting ahead." It tends to affect both the incentive to produce food or other goods for market sale and the incentive to sell labor in the market. Beyond the allowance for a small measure of personal profit just large enough to meet a limited individual goal—the conclusion of bridewealth payments or the purchase of a bicycle, a flashlight, or a new pair of shoes—the possession of extra cash is interpreted by the Mossi as surplus. Pressure is strong to redistribute it, or to use it to increase participation in the reciprocal system through generous gifts to kinsmen and friends.

The relation of migratory labor to the Mossi economy provides still another example of the difficulty of reconciling market exchange with the processes of redistribution and reciprocity. For again, although the goods a man acquires through the sale of his labor are regarded as his personal property, his kinsmen still have some claim to them. This is especially true of the money earned and the goods acquired by young men who work away from Yatenga as migrant laborers during the important rainy months when they are needed on their families' farms. They compensate their kinsmen for the loss of their labor with gifts of money and goods sent back by returning workers or by mail, or the compensation is paid when the workers themselves return to their homeland after several seasons away. As long as migrant workers indirectly fulfill their obligation to contribute to the economic well-being of the kin group, their place in the redistributive system remains secure and the web of reciprocal ties which unites them with their community remains intact.

However, lacking any special training, the position of Mossi workers in the market for unskilled laborers in Ghana, the Ivory Coast, and the cities of the Western Sudan is too uncertain and not potentially rewarding enough for Mossi to forfeit their security in relation to their kinsmen in their homeland by refusing to fulfill their obligations there.

Failure to participate in the redistributive system as it operates within the context of the kin group not only places the Mossi's assurance of future economic support in jeopardy, but also elicits the vociferously expressed disapproval of all his family. And often of the community as well. Thus the pleasure an individual may feel in keeping for himself—refusing to share, a newly acquired object, such as a shirt or a bicycle acquired through the market, will be offset by the social pressures he will suffer. For he has violated a value basic to Mossi culture, one that defines the social, emotional, and economic subordination of the individual to the lineage as an essential virtue. The man who fails to share with his kinsmen ceases to be a worthy and reliable member of the kin group. He threatens its collective security and angers the ancestral spirits.

Sometimes it is possible to defer the obligation to share with the lineage. If, for example, a man is known to have earned some money from the sale of his tobacco crop, he can refuse the request of a kinsman for a loan by explaining he wants to invest the money earned in the purchase of kola nuts. This will be accepted. However, when the kola nuts have been obtained and resold for a profit in the local market, the person whose request for financial assistance was refused earlier has a right to part of the profits. Or a man may decline a kinsman's request for monetary aid with the explanation that he is saving money to buy a bicycle. When the bicycle is purchased, the kinsman who was denied assistance earlier has a special right to its use.

The cause-and-effect relation is circular. Because the strength of pressure for participation in the redistributive and reciprocal spheres of the economy is strong, participation in the market cannot function as an adequately secure economic alternative unless the individual separates himself almost entirely from his kinsmen and his community. In fact this is what most economically successful Mossi entrepreneurs must do, cut themselves off from their families and friends. The few full-time merchants in any Mossi market are almost always men who have left their own villages and allowed their ties to the patriclan to lapse. Usually such assertion of independence from the traditional social system is accompanied by conversion to Islam which, to some extent, serves to provide ideological justification for the abandonment of customary economic and social behavior.

For the majority of Mossi, however, participation in the market persists as peripheral to the means by which they maintain their economic security and peripheral to the process by which they allocate their goods.

In the instance of part-time market entrepreneurs the necessity of making such a complete break can often be avoided by activation of the bond-friend relationship. As an example it serves further to point up the dilemma the Mossi face when they are tempted to widen their participation in the market. Outside the kinship system it is the bond-friend relationship that serves as the most frequent alternative to economic interaction with members of the patriclan. The voluntary association between bond-friends provides the basis for an economic alliance lacking the diffuse obligations characteristic of kinship ties. A nonkinsman is especially preferable as a partner in personal enterprises not requiring group effort and where money profit provides the motivation. Consequently private economic plans are more often entered into with a bond-friend than with a kinsman, and valuable personal property is frequently stored in a bond-friend's house. For a man is less fearful of revealing personal wealth to a nonkinsman with whom he is not required to share.

Although a bond-friend may be asked for assistance with farm work, these days his help is more likely to be sought for a commercial enterprise, such as the weaving of cotton cloth into bands. These may be sold on the local market or in a neighboring community, but they are more commonly taken south to the forest areas of Ghana and the Ivory Coast where cotton goods command a higher price. The money earned is often used to import kola nuts, which bring a good price in Yatenga, where they are widely used as a stimulant. Two bond-friends either work together on every aspect of such an endeavor or divide the labor, one taking the responsibility for weaving the bands, the other for marketing them. A portion of the shared profits is often used for further investment. Every effort is made to keep their stores and their profits secret. This is facilitated by the fact that at least part of their activity occurs outside the local community and by the practice of placing their goods in one another's houses where they can be kept away from the interested eyes of their own fellow kinsmen.

For these several reasons it is possible, and very important to identify the market among the Mossi as being of peripheral rather than primal importance in the organization of their economic system. Land, the basic productive good, does not enter the market at all. Only surplus subsistence commodities and surplus labor are available there. The only goods for which the market serves as the principal means of exchange are luxuries like matches, mirrors, soap, and European cloth.

So far the role of the Mossi market as a locus for the activation of redistributive and reciprocal ties is nearly as important as its function in providing a mechanism for the adjustment through reallocation by sale of small surpluses of labor and subsistence goods.

As long as land does not enter the Mossi markets—and so long as working the land persists as the technological basis of Mossi culture—the markets are likely to retain their peripheral role in the economy. But once land is sold, the Mossi can lose the means of making a living as farmers. When that occurs, they will have to market their labor in order to purchase the goods they need to live. At that point the transformation of their economic system will be underway.

So far the persistence of the traditional form of Mossi technology has impeded such a transformation. For the technology has sustained the indigenous social system based on kinship. This, in turn, has served to perpetuate ancestor worship, and while the ancestors remain powerful, their descendants are unlikely to risk separating themselves from the land.

CHAPTER FIVE

SOCIAL ORGANIZATION

The relation between Mossi social organization and the economic system just described is one of total integration. Each structures the other, and they are mutually dependent for the fulfillment of their respective functions.

KINSHIP

The Lineage System

Kinship provides the basic organizing principle in Mossi society, and it is the patrilineal descent system that is fundamental to the organization of kinship. So it is with patrilineality that a description of Mossi kinship must begin.

Succession not only to economic but also to social, political, and religious status are all determined by a system of patrilineal descent in which the exogamous totemic patrisib, *booyalengo*, is the largest unit. The component lineages, *boodoose,* of the sib provide the core of agnatic kinsmen who, together with their wives and children, comprise the membership of the compound residential kin group, the patriclan, *saka*. The typically dispersed compound dwellings of each patriclan contain a number of polygynous extended or joint families which are further segmented into several polygynous and nuclear family groups. Adjustment between the land, technology, the economy, and family size and organization is maintained by the constantly operating process of segmentary fission. The dynamically supple integration of the several units within the patriclan provides the Mossi with a variety of sources of economic, social, emotional, and supernatural support. Acceptance of his clearly defined responsibilities in relation to the system assures his personal security.

Membership in the sib is determined on the basis of a shared tradition of common patrilineal descent and maintained by economic and social cooperation, exogamy, and recognition of the authority of the sib and lineage elders. Such organization is ritually reinforced by veneration of the spirits of the founding ancestors and observance of prohibitions regarding the sib totem.

Most Mossi are ignorant of all but the chronologically most recent and relevant details of their genealogies. Memory rarely serves an elder accurately beyond the generation of father's father. The attitude of the Mossi toward this genealogical ignorance, despite the attention they give to kinship, is reflective of the functional unimportance, perhaps even the functional advantage, of such ignorance. When asked, young men usually suggest hopefully that their fathers know the names of their ancestors. When their fathers are asked in turn, they usually respond with the familiar Mossi assertion *tonde patoin mi ye*, "we cannot know," a response which is not intended to be evasive, and one which is, in fact, accurate.

For the Mossi believe it is dangerous to utter the name of a powerful supernatural being, just as it would be dangerously presumptuous for a small child to refer to an elder kinsman by name. Such impertinence toward an elder member of the patriclan, or a still older ancestral spirit, would attract their angry attention and possible punishment. Consequently the names of deceased members of the descent group must not be uttered. If they have recently died and are regarded as still intimately and immediately involved in the affairs of their survivors, literally hovering about the household, they are referred to as "shade person," *masam soba,* but never by their proper name. If they have been dead for a longer period but within the memory of adults, they are referred to as "father," *baba,* collectively as "the fathers," *banamba,* or as "grandfather," *yaba,* or "the grandfathers," *yaba namba.* This last term is used for the spirits of all ancestors who belong to or precede the generation of father's father. The putative apical ancestor of the sib is called simply "founding ancestor."

This is how ancestral spirits are addressed on ritual occasions. Consequently their names cannot be learned by the younger members of the kin group. Once those who knew them when they were alive have died, the ancestors' names are totally forgotten.[1]

However the strength of the bond of common descent in the sib is not weakened in any way by the absence of an accurate genealogical record. In fact its vagueness probably provides the descent system with useful flexibility. The record is sufficiently accurate to validate and sanction relations between the living, but not so rigid that occasionally necessary genealogical adjustments are ever likely to threaten lineage continuity.

Within the component lineages of the sib, where cohesion is most vital, the living members rarely belong to more than three generations. The fact of their common descent is recorded in the memory of the elders who, of course, knew their fathers and their fathers' fathers and can attest with equal accuracy to the paternity of all their living descendants. Thus, in the group within which the maintenance of solidarity is most crucial, cohesion is closely supported by precise genealogical records. And conversely, within the necessarily and usefully looser organization of the sib the vagueness of the record provides for an equally useful lack of rigidity.

The economic ties that unite all members of the sib are activated most vigorously and continuously within its component lineages. First there is the fact of collective ownership of land by all agnates, the spirits of their ancestors, and the future generations of their descendants. Only through membership in the sib can the Mossi acquire the right to land use, and only through proper land use can they retain this right. This requires adherence to traditionally

---

1. With one exception: The names of historically important members of noble lineages are often recalled in the songs of praise singers.

sanctioned patterns of land tenure—those established by the ancestors, assured by training, and reinforced by the elders.

Conflict over the allocation of work, land, and economic goods is controlled by the strong positive value attached to cooperation within the kin group and, when necessary, by the mediation of lineage leaders. The first responsibility of the Mossi adult is to behave in his economic and social activities in a manner that contributes to the stability and continuity of his kin group. The principle that supports this is not selflessness but self-interest: The well-being of the kin group is the best assurance of the individual's well-being and of societal stability. In fact, of course, conflict and competition are as characteristic of interaction between Mossi kinsmen as are amity and cooperation. Naturally the closer the tie and the more intense the economic and social interaction, the more frequent is the likelihood of dispute. Thus most conflict among the Mossi occurs within the societal unit best organized to deal with it—the kin group. The important implications of this fact for an understanding of the Mossi political system will be taken up in the next chapter.

The social power of the sib elder, *ni kiema,* the ultimate source of authority in the kinship system, is derived from three sources: from his role as the guardian of the collective and individual rights of the descent group and all its members, from his status as sacerdotal intermediary between his kinsmen and their ancestral spirits, and from his political position as counselor to the village chief.

Typically the authority of the sib elder is most often exercized in the regulation of affairs in his own patriclan; more occasionally it is called upon in the adjustment of relations between the component lineages of the sib. Otherwise his power is held in reserve as the ultimate source of control in the kinship-based social system and as the symbolic representation of the conservative will of the ancestors—*yaba soore,* "the grandfather's way," the traditionally based, supernaturally sanctioned guide to proper action in the present.

Sib exogamy serves to maintain the integrity of the descent group and, indirectly, to assure the useful extension of affinal ties. It is strictly observed. Whenever a marriage is projected, the ancestry of both partners must be carefully examined. The discussions of genealogy that this precipitates provide a further means of maintaining awareness of sib affiliation and are of particular importance in this way when the component lineages of the sib are dispersed in several villages. Attention to the observance of the exogamous prohibition is the responsibility of the elders. Young people themselves are rarely acquainted personally with more than a few of the members of their descent group outside the local community, but by means of these discussions they come gradually to learn the full extent of their agnatic ties both within and beyond the village. Violation of the exogamous rule is, of course, regarded as incest.

Veneration of the apical ancestors of the sib, who punish incest, provides a still further means of perpetuating awareness of patrilineal relationship. The spirits of these first ancestors dwell in the vicinity of the residence of the founding lineage of the sib. The *ro kiengo*, "important old house," the shrine at which they are worshipped, is located within its walls. Usually only local members of the sib assist at the ritual propitiation of these more remote ancestors. But on important ceremonial occasions the first sacrifices are made to them in the presence of the elders of all the locally established lineages of the sib. Then the same ceremony is observed successively, and in order of seniority, at the shrine located in the compound residence of each lineage.

Observance of the sib totem also serves as a ritual means of reinforcing solidarity, cohesion, and awareness of common descent among the members of the sib. All agnatic kinsmen are abjured from harming the animal, *kitame*, usually identified with an important event related to the founding of their descent group.

In the sib that has the finch as its totem, for example, it is said that their first ancestor had been wandering lost in the bush and was lying collapsed and near death from thirst when a finch moistened his lips with water. The bird then led him to a spring where he was refreshed and able to find his way back to his kinsmen. He told them how he had been saved from death and enjoined them always to regard the finch as their benefactor and never to harm it. They obeyed him and instructed their children to do so as well. When they died and became ancestral spirits, they continued to enforce the prohibition by sending sickness to any of their descendants who violated it.

Another sib, with the crocodile as its totem, has the tradition that its ancestors used to hide in the crocodile's nest during enemy raids on their village. In grateful recognition of this refuge they instructed their descendants not to harm the animal.

The Mossi sib always bears the name of the compound residence of the founding lineage, which is usually taken from some peculiarity of the locale, a hillock or rock formation or a distinctive cluster of trees. In describing his kinship affiliation, a man ordinarily mentions only the name of his patriclan residence. If he wants to be more explicit, he may append the name of the residence of the founding lineage of his sib. If it is located in another village, a full description of his kinship affiliation would entail mention of the name of the sib, the village in which it is located, the name of his own village, the name of his village sector, and the name of his own patriclan residence. Thus if the residence of the founding lineage of a man's sib, called Togeh, were located in the village of Gambo, while his own lineage name were Tilimbugurey and were located in the sector called Warema of the village of Gourcy, he would identify his kinship status by saying that he belonged to Gambo Togeh, Gourcy Warema Tilimbugurey.

The Patriclan (Saka)

As a consequence of the continuous process of segmentary fission the lineages that comprise the sib are typically dispersed in several neighboring villages. This separation inhibits extensive economic and social interaction between them and explains the fact that the corporate functions of the Mossi sib are less important in the daily life of the individual, the kin group, and the community than are those of the lineages of which it is comprised. Even when the founding lineage of the sib is established locally, the component lineages are always spatially, economically, socially, politically, and ritually semiautonomous. For each provides the core of agnatic male kinsmen who together with their wives and children comprise the principal membership of a separate residential kin group, the patriclan, *saka*.[2]

2. I take my use of the term clan from Murdock (George Peter Murdock, *Social Structure*, New York: Macmillan, 1949, Chapter 4), and intend it to denote a residential kin group which is comprised of all the localized male members of the lineage, their unmarried female agnates, and the wives of the married males.

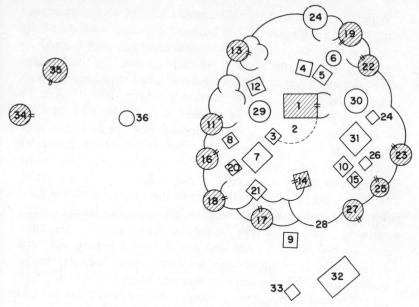

A small patriclan residence, *saka*

Because common residence is basic to the operation of the patriclan as a corporate entity, a description of the physical layout of the
compound patriclan dwelling serves best as a means of introducing
discussion of the activities—both internal, in relation to the several
smaller kin group units within it, and external, in relation to the
larger community—that justify the assessment of the role of the
patriclan as equivalent to that of the descent group as a unit of
primary importance for an understanding of the organization of
Mossi kinship.

Typically the houses in the Mossi patriclan residence are clustered
around the household of the lineage elder, *sak kasama,* whose own
house and courtyard, surrounded by the dwellings of his wives,
forms the core of the residence of his own polygamous family. If
he has only recently succeeded to the role of elder, his sons' households probably remain in the part of the compound residence where
he also lived prior to his succession to his new position. The rest of
the living space within the walls of the compound dwelling is taken
up by the clusters of houses of the various patrilocal extended
families of the elders' younger brothers.

With the exception of a newly married woman who often resides temporarily in the house of her husband's mother, married adults of both sexes live in separate individual dwellings each fronted by a private courtyard, the walls of which are formed by the contiguous houses and courtyards of other wives or co-wives, husbands or brothers, and their wives and married sons and their families.

In addition to the separate dwellings of all residents of the clan, and the granaries which are usually located near the houses of their respective owners, there are two other structures of particular importance to the organization of the clan residence. One is the grinding platform which serves as the women's gathering place. The other is the sun shelter. The role of the sun shelter as the focal point of masculine cohesiveness in the clan has already been mentioned. It is there that the men of the lineage gather to take their meals, work at odd jobs, rest and gossip. And it is there also that they receive male visitors—agnates from other lineages, affinal kinsmen, bond-friends, agemates, and neighbors.

These two structures, the grinding platform of the women and the sun shelter of the men, are symbolic of a cleavage basic to the organization of the patriclan, one that results from the complementary distinctions of consanguineal and affinal kinship, the twin principles from which clan structure and function are derived. As has been noted, young boys are encouraged to join their elder male kinsmen under the sun shelter from the time they can walk, but only very small girls are welcome there, and then rarely. Usually they are sent away—to help their mothers at the kitchen fire or at the grinding platform.

The fact of sex difference is more important than that of lineage affiliation, and this easy association with the agnatic kin group ceases for a little girl soon after she is able to move about on her own. Then she is assigned her first tasks in her mother's household. Quickly thereafter she becomes so occupied caring for her smaller brothers and sisters and assisting her mother at gathering firewood and food that she is effectively cut off from extensive interaction with her male kinsmen. This separation of the female members of the lineage which begins in early childhood is likely to persist until old age, when, widowed and past the age of childbearing, a woman can return from her deceased husband's patriclan residence and live out her last years with the members of her own lineage. Then

"... the sun shelter ... focal point of masculine cohesiveness in the patriclan ..."

her senior status and effective sexlessness justify the appellation assigned her. She is called "elder brother," *ba rawa*.

For the Mossi male no such breaks occur in the continuity of his interaction with his lineage. For him the clan residence of his father is usually his home for life.

The house, *da koorey rogo,* of the unmarried young men of the lineage is always located just outside the common exterior wall of the patriclan residence. Before he marries, a young man builds himself a separate house, outside the walls, but close to his father's residence. When he marries, the wall is broken and his house and courtyard are joined on to the patriclan dwelling.

Uusually succession to an important new status in the lineage is accompanied by a shift in residence. Thus when a man succeeds to the status of patriclan elder, he moves into the house previously occupied by his deceased elder brother. The elder's granaries and their contents are taken over as well. If the deceased elder's wives remain as part of his successor's household, they keep their houses. Those who move to the households of their sons or return to their own lineages abandon their dwellings to the wives of the man who succeeds to the role of their deceased husband as patriclan elder. A similar shift in residence follows the death of the head of an extended family.

The Extended Family (Yiri)

Except when it stands alone as the immediate and usually temporary consequence of lineage fission, the extended family is always spatially, economically, socially, and ritually a part of the patriclan. Ordinarily it is composed of a man and his wives, his young children, and his married sons and their families. Occasionally it may also contain the polygynous household of one or more of his younger siblings. The Mossi extended family is most important as an economically cooperating group and as a unit of descent and inheritance, both of which are determined by seniority on a generational basis. The houses of the members of the extended family are usually clustered together within the larger aggregation of dwellings that comprise the patriclan.

Fields under the direct proprietorship of the father or eldest brother are worked together cooperatively. The product which results, like the crops stored in the granaries of the lineage elder, are used for the support not only of the household of the family head, but also of any members of the extended family in need. As with lineage and sib elders, this usage balances the fact that a man's inherited land holdings are likely to be most extensive at a time in his life when most of his sons have established their own households and the size of his own elementary family and its subsistence needs are actually reduced. Rights to the use of all other land are distributed individually among the adult members of the component polygynous and elementary families and worked by them according to the pattern already described. The head of the extended family acts as intermediary between his younger kinsmen and the elders of the lineage and sib. He does not, however, have any formal ceremonial role and is unable himself to propitiate directly the ancestral spirits.

Generally, with the death of the extended family head it is preferred that the group persist as a fraternal joint family. But, although this pattern is preferred by the Mossi, it rarely occurs. The far more frequent consequence has already been indicated: The younger sons leave the original patriclan residence if their share in their father's legacy is inadequate to meet their needs. They move out to set up an independent household for themselves, one which has initially the structure of a fraternal joint family. If the move is permanent, relations with the parent lineage decrease because of distance and the fact that the emerging kin group has acquired new land. With time, and especially if the distance from the parent lineage is great, social and economic interaction become less and less intensive and the new kin group becomes more and more involved with its new neighbors in the new community of which it is becoming a part.

The diminution of the means of reinforcing redistributive and reciprocal economic ties through constant contact is paralleled by a gradual decrease in participation in the ceremonials that accompany the worship of lineage ancestors. In the first phase of separation the eldest member of the new residential kin group returns to the compound residence of the parent lineage to make sacrifices on important cremonial occasions. In the second phase these sacrifices are made on the road leading back to the home village. And finally they are abandoned altogether as the descendants of the recently

established group begin to make their requests for supernatural
support to the spirits of their own deceased founders. After several
generations the senior male's role evolves into that of lineage elder;
he assumes the political role of village counselor in the new community and the ceremonial responsibility of acting as intermediary
with the ancestral spirits. Gradually the traditional pattern of resi-
rence re-emerges. As new houses are added and mature sons marry,
the structure of the patriclan reappears and a new lineage has
developed within the sib.

When such separation results from a quarrel, which usually
occurs as the result of a dispute over inheritance between a man's
brothers and his sons, the dissident group that moves away to
establish a new residence is called *boo bilegum bilegum*. The term
means literally "kin calm," *bilegum bilegum* being a phrase used to
soothe a frustrated infant or child. Applied to the new kin group
resulting from conflict within the lineage, it implies recognition that
the tension between the two groups may result in a permanent
break and that both must behave with caution in order to avoid
a total schism. Spatial separation of the sib membership always
results in a decrease in economic, social, and ceremonial interaction.
If it is accompanied by a serious rupture of amity, the bond of
kinship may break altogether. When this occurs a new sib emerges.

The Nuclear Family (Zaka)

The monogamous marriage relationship provides the basis for
the smallest unit in the Mossi kinship system, the nuclear family,
zaka. Although monogamy is necessarily the norm, polygyny is
preferred. However the ratio of the sexes appears to be roughly
equal, and despite the fact that Mossi girls marry shortly after
puberty, and men not until their middle or late twenties, marriage
is usually monogamous during the first years. For the average
Mossi one wife in his young manhood, and possibly a second when
he has inherited a position of greater importance in the kin group, is
the pattern. It is only a few older men of high status who can
acquire the wealth necessary to collect an extensive number of
wives.

Marriage is forbidden, of course, within the sib and with a member of mother's patrilineage, with a leper, or with a person guilty of bestiality or descended from a person guilty of this crime.[3]

Both the levirate and the sororate are observed by the Mossi. However a widow beyond the age of childbearing may take up residence with an adult son, or if she has no grown sons she may return to reside with her own patriclan. Thus the levirate functions only in the instance of the younger, sexually and economically more productive wives of a deceased man. Although the sororate is also observed, the sanctions are weaker. Sororal polygyny occurs only in the instance of twins.

The Mossi marriage relationship is established gradually. A girl first receives gifts in exchange for her sexual favors and is expected in turn to perform small tasks for her lover. These begin with bringing him warm water with which to bathe after intercourse. When the liaison has become somewhat more permanent, she takes a gift of cooked food to his house the following day. If he is married, she may take a present of sauce or spices to his wife. Such exchange marks the first stage of the economic and social cooperation, reinforced by sexual gratification, that may ultimately develop into marriage. The young man's senior kinsmen notice what is occurring and have a chance to check the young girl's family connections to see that the possible union will not be incestuous, to investigate the reputation of her family for training their daughters to be good wives, and to find out informally if her kinsmen are likely to be agreeable to the marriage. If the prospects appear to be good, negotiations are formalized.

The young man's father and the men of his generation act as intermediaries between him and the kinsmen of his intended wife. They visit and take gifts to the bride's mother and to the elders of her lineage. If these presents are adequate—usually they involve gifts of millet, livestock, money, and objects of European manufacture such as metal cooking utensils and cloth—the girl is prepared to

3.   While homosexuality appears to be almost nonexistent among the Mossi, bestiality involving burros is generally known and widely abhored. It appears to develop as a consequence of the adolescent experiments of young herdsmen who have not yet been circumcised and are thus denied access to women. When this behavior recurs in adulthood it is believed to be the consequence of a curse. The guilty man is divorced and must find a new wife from among women whose ancestors have committed the same crime.

join the young man in his patriclan residence. She is groomed by her mother and equipped with kitchen equipment and new clothes and waits for the arrival of her husband's brothers. After a mock battle between them and her younger siblings, who protest jokingly that she is too valuable to be lost for the sake of the meager bride-wealth received, she is taken off to her husband's residence.

The economic activities of a Mossi man and his wife or wives—the allocation of farmland, the organization of work and the maintenance of household property—have already been described. It is necessary only to add that these economic functions transcend in importance the social role of the nuclear or polygynous family. Social and emotional contact between a man and his wife is minimal. Their relationship is essentially economic and sexual. They live separately, eat separately, travel separately, and participate in both social and religious ceremonies independently of one another. Even at the work in which they cooperate their tasks are more often coordinated than accomplished together.

In the cultivation of their fields and at the harvests, where they do work side by side, they are separated by an emotional distance that has its origins in the early and differing enculturative experience of boys and girls and is reinforced by economic and social separation sustained throughout their lives. This sexually differentiated enculturation results in the emergence of two personality types so different that there is neither the motivation nor the possibility for much close contact between them. Mossi men perceive the personality of their women as being in an absolute sense different from that of men. Consequently it is assumed that emotional or intellectual closeness between the sexes, even if it were regarded as desirable, would be impossible to achieve.

This separation characterizes their sexual relations as well. Before marriage a man compensates his sexual partners for their favors with presents. After marriage compliance is a wifely duty. This absolves men from responsibility to gratify women sexually. Foreplay is brief and limited to the man's efforts to force the girl to permit penetration as soon as possible. The likelihood that she will remain unsatisfied may be increased by the neurological damage she has already incurred as a result of the cliterodictomy. It is possible that this absence of satisfactory sexual adjustment may be related to the recalcitrance and intractability widely regarded by

Mossi men as female personality characteristics. In any case this attitude completes the vicious circle.[4]

A man who has recently married and is unable to provide his wife with a house of her own lodges her with his mother. There she assists her husband's mother with her household tasks and visits her husband only at night and at his request. She prepares his food and carries it out to the sun shelter where he continues to take his meals and his ease among his male kinsmen. Husband and wife make their visits to their separate kinsmen and friends alone. Although they cooperate in marketing their produce, they do not attend the market together. All ceremonial occasions are attended separately also, usually in the company of their bond-friends of the same sex.

Thus in farm work, the maintenance of the household, and even in sexual relations, behavior between husband and wife is set by custom and determines their expectations and actions toward one another to an extent that makes a minimum of actual communication necessary. Consequently a man's verbal exchange with his wife is limited largely to the instructions he gives her and criticism with the manner in which she carries them out. In a sense this absence of emotional intimacy and involvement between husband and wife functions to minimize marital conflict by minimizing contact itself and the limited expectations of the marriage partners reduce the potential for frustration.

Children

Although parents in the polygynous or nuclear family are the first source of support for children, the education and social experience—particularly of male children—occurs most significantly within the more diffuse context of the extended family and patriclan. The relationship of boys to the other male members of

4. It is also possible, and this is pure speculation, that the lack of an intact clitoris may make more generalized arousal necessary. As such arousal is not provided by foreplay, repeated penetration may serve to achieve the same effect. Anyhow the Mossi men report their women require repeated intercourse within a very short period in order to be satisfied. And Mossi men are proud of their ability to provide for this. The absence of need for a sustained erection prior to penetration may facilitate the male in meeting his partner's requirements.

their lineage is especially close. As adults their closest contact both within the kin group and in the community is with their patrilineal kinsmen of the same age. With them they share the performance of most economic tasks, as well as similar roles in the social and ceremonial life of the patriclan.

As soon as a boy is able to walk he goes off to play or work with other boys, and he takes his meals and finds comfort among the gathering of elder kinsmen almost always to be found under the sun shelter. At puberty he leaves his father's household to live in the young men's house outside the walls of the patriclan residence.

A result of this early enculturation within the patriclan is the diffusion of the field upon which the child depends for social and emotional security. For males, at least, the emotional depth of relationship to biological parents is unlikely to be much greater than it is to other members of the agnatic kin group. In early childhood the strictness of the behavior of his father and mother, who have the chief responsibility for discipline, can be compensated for by escape to the more permissive context of a relationship with a man of father's father's generation. A child out of favor with one kinsman can always quickly find comfort from another. For Mossi males, who live out their entire lives within the supportive ambience of the patriclan, the result of this experience appears to be a personality whose sources of security are both shallow and diffuse.

Young girls also learn early that the kin group is the ultimate source of their security. Both in the performance of their tasks and in the acceptance of male authority, they are taught from the first that they must subordinate their interests to those of the lineage. This early training in the acceptance of authority and in the efficient performance of assigned tasks is important in order that they make good wives. A lineage that gains a reputation for improper training of its girls is soon unable to find them husbands and thus risks the loss of the opportunity of using the marriage of its daughters to establish or reinforce profitable alliances.

Consequently any deviation from what is regarded as proper behavior on the part of a young girl is promptly and radically dealt with. The treatment of a girl at Gourcy who stole some money from her father illustrates this. She had used the money to take her small friends to market and buy them all new headcloths. Her

". . . the education and social experience—particularly of male children—occurs most significantly within the more diffused context of the extended family and patriclan."

sudden prosperity, generosity, and chic were noticed by the villagers
and reported to her kinsmen. When she confessed to the theft she
was taken to the entrance of the patriclan residence and staked out
on the ground "like a goat," as the Mossi said. There she was left
sobbing throughout the day. This treatment was intended by her
kinsmen not only as punishment, but as a means of avoiding
the reputation of poorly training their daughters for marriage
by demonstrating publicly that they did not condone such
comportment.

The concern manifested by the lineage for the actions of its
members derives from the fact that in relation to the community
any member represents the group. This explains the harshness with
which delinquency is dealt with within the lineage. And it also
explains the stern interest parents take in the behavior of their
children. For, within the kin group it is the parents who are
primarily responsible for the training of the next generation of
adults.

Despite this concern with the education of the young, the early
phases of the Mossi child's enculturative experience are characterized by an absence of compulsion. A usual aspect of any Mossi
gathering is the group of young boys and girls quietly accompanying their elders about their tasks and gently being encouraged to
listen and observe carefully all that is taking place. From infancy
the right to participate in the activities of the elders is dependent
upon obedience and self-control. A child in arms is carried forward
at a ceremonial and urged to watch all that occurs so long as he
remains quiet. If he cries, he is taken away until he stops. A noisy
older child is slapped rudely and sent away, but allowed later to
creep quietly and unobtrusively back. This establishes a pattern
that is to characterize the Mossi's means of adjustment to his kinsmen throughout life—subordination results in acceptance and
security, insubordination means exclusion and isolation.

Affinal Ties

In addition to its relations with other lineages within the sib each
localized patrilineal descent group exists at the center of an intricate
network of affinally established ties which may unite it with
nearly every other descent group in the community, thus binding

almost the entire village together on the basis of either consanguineal or affinal relations. Because marriages are also contracted with members of kin groups in neighboring communities, usually those closest by, kinship provides the basis for cooperative economic, social, and political interaction over a field that is usually coterminous in its dimensions with the extent of individual and group needs for such cooperation.

seems circular

An important function of Mossi marriage is the establishment or reinforcement of these ties. Economic cooperation between affinally related kin groups does not require mutual aid in the performance of tasks, but rather it implies agreement not to disrupt or compete with one another's economic interests. If conflict between in-laws arises, it should be quickly settled because of this important agreement. The value of perpetuating the cooperative and amicable relation between affinally related kin groups is manifested in the importance attached to institutionalized means of controlling marital discord.

Perhaps most important among these is the avoidance relationship between a man and his wife's mother. The Mossi recognize that a man's mother-in-law is both his most likely adversary and his closest potential ally in his relationship with his wife, and, by extension, in his and his kinsmens' relations with her patriclan and lineage. For it is his wife's mother who loses an important economic aide and a close companion when her daughter marries. She is most likely to be grieved at the loss of her daughter and least likely to be satisfied with the marriage presents made in compensation. She is also most likely to be the first to hear of her daughter's troubles in her new household and, if not otherwise dissuaded, most likely to make her son-in-law's domestic difficulties worse. He needs to stay in her good graces. To maximize the potential amicability of this relationship, he must minimize the possibility of conflict. He does this by avoiding her.

analogous in months of Mossi?

When an exchange of messages or goods is necessary it is accomplished by means of an intermediary, very often his bond-friend or a fellow age mate belonging to his wife's or his wife's mother's agnatic kin group. If he inadvertently meets his wife's mother, he should avoid taking notice of her. If he cannot do this without appearing rude, he must stop and greet her formally. If, for example, he meets her on a pathway outside the village, he should try to hide or take another path without being noticed. She should do the same. However, if each knows that he has been seen by the other, they must both approach to within a few yards, place whatever they are carrying on the ground, kneel with the upper part of the body resting forward on the forearms, snap their fingers in the conventional Mossi sign of deference and respect, and exchange a highly formalized set of salutations—so formalized that they allow for no variation or the introduction of other topics of conversation. Each should then rise and be quickly on his way, often continuing the exchange of formal greetings until out of earshot. Thus when face-to-face contact cannot be wholly avoided it is limited to such highly formalized exchange that no issue that might result in conflict can arise.

A woman's relationship with her husband's mother obviously cannot be as formalized. For the fact of patrilocal residence alone results in a necessarily greater frequency of interaction. However the differences in their age and status result in a degree of social and emotional separation that inhibits intimacy between them in a manner that also serves to minimize the possibility of conflict. A young woman must always listen respectfully to her husband's mother and must not assert herself in her presence. This reduces the chances for the development of the sort of casual conversation between equals that might result in the emergence of controversial subjects that could lead to an open expression of hostility.

A woman is expected to behave with similar respect and deference toward the other members of her husband's agnatic kin group. Within the patriclan residence her own closest social and emotional ties are likely to be with her children and with other wives of her own generation. Outside her husband's kin group her closest ties remain with the members of her own patriclan and lineage and with her own bond-friends and age mates.

The converse of the relationship varying from formality to the point of near-total avoidance that characterizes the behavior of each marriage partner to the parents of the other is found in their relationship to one another's younger siblings. Here the broadest joking is permitted without the possibility of offense. When a man's younger siblings come into the presence of his wife, she is expected to insult them, to seek in a humorous way to deride them, to criticize their behavior, their appearance, their lack of energy and skill at their work, and their general stupidity. This also provides her with an indirect means of criticizing her husband himself. By saving her grievance until she has a visit from one of his younger siblings, she can, within the context of joking, pour out her resentment at the way she is treated and may reveal the causes of her dissatisfaction with his behavior. In return his younger siblings can answer with hostile jocular banter of the same sort, conveying to her both her husband's and their fellow kinsmen's dissatisfaction. They also can be relied on to relay to her husband what she has said. If he recognizes as valid the criticism implied within her joking remarks, he may act to rectify those aspects of his behavior that are frustrating to her and thereby threatening to the stability of their marriage.

A man has the same relationship with the younger siblings of his wife. He also may wait for a visit from them in order to express within the socially acceptable context of joking the grievances he might not express directly toward her or her other kinsmen. In this manner the joking relationship provides both marriage partners with an indirect means of achieving catharsis of their feelings of frustration and, at the same time, communication of the sources of their dissatisfaction. This makes possible their rectification and contributes to the likelihood of avoiding future tension.

In addition to the culturally defined responsibility of each marriage partner to avoid, through one variety of indirection or another, a conflict with the kinsmen of the other, the Mossi man and wife are also pressured by their respective kin groups to maintain good marital relations with one another. This pressure is likely to come from the man's lineage. For three reasons: to avoid forfeiture of the marriage presents which might follow from the dissolution of the marriage if it were the husband's fault, to assure the perpetuation of the cooperative tie with the patrilineage of the wife, and to maintain the good reputation of the kin group in the community so that their other sons will be able to contract favorable marriages.

Similarly the bride's kinsmen are likely to exert pressure on her to conform with the cultural expectations of a wife. For if she fails to do so, not only will her kinsmen be required to return the marriage presents they have received, but, more seriously, they will risk acquiring a reputation for failing to prepare their daughters properly to assume the responsibilities of marriage.

Divorce

When hostility grows so great that it can no longer be dealt with through these culturally acceptable channels or avoided by institutionalized means, commitment to the preservation of the marriage is abandoned, and its dissolution soon follows. Failure of the agnatic kinsmen of either partner to intervene in order to end marital conflict is perceived as an indication that the marriage is no longer regarded as a valuable or viable link between the two kin groups involved.

Because achieving a bond of amity and cooperation between lineages and clans is one of the principal social functions of marriage, when it becomes evident that such a bond no longer exists the marriage itself ceases to be of value. Consequently support for other marriages uniting the two kin groups is likely to be weakened also. Once this occurs, disintegration of conflict into open hostility often develops quickly. Grievances are not rectified, and one marriage partner or the other soon provides grounds for a formal break. A man may refuse to supply his wife with millet from his granary or she may fail to show him proper deference before his kinsmen. Left unattended, the rift gradually widens. Soon she will leave his household to return to her own patriclan where another marriage can be arranged for her—one that serves her kinsmen's interests better by establishing in some other part of the community a new cooperative tie to replace the one that has been lost.

Complementary Filiation

The affinal tie that links the respective lineages of a child's parents is useful, in a particular way, to the child himself. For mother's patrilineage constitutes the most important alternative source of support to that provided by the agnatic kin group. And residence with mother's patriclan is the preferred alternative to patrilocality. *Yasenamba,* the term used to describe this group, means literally "the lying ones." According to the Mossi the term refers to the fact that if a child's mother "had been a man" the child would be a member of their lineage. But because this is not so, they are only "lying" when they act toward him as if he were agnatically related. This lesser formality is also used to explain the more permissive behavior that characterizes a Mossi's relationship to his mother's lineage.

To compensate for the absence of legal rights among his "lying" kinsmen, he is permitted to steal from them, particularly from his mother's brother, his special "lying person," *ya soba*. He can also steal a portion of the food prepared for his mother's brother's funeral. In both instances he takes advantage of the permissiveness of the relationship to subvert its legal limitations. To control his sister's son's behavior, mother's brother usually gives him an animal from time to time, a goat or a sheep to "shame him" and prevent him from stealing property at his funeral that belongs rightfully to the mother's brother's own children. A joking relationship with mother's brother's wives serves both to reduce their frustrations with ego's occasional depredations of their husband's property and as a means of control, for they may indicate within the "inoffensive" context of joking the limits of their toleration.

As an adult a man often acts as intermediary between his mother's brother's children and their father. In fear of his punishment they may flee to father's sister's son for protection and ask him to intervene in seeking their parent's forgiveness. Similarly a sister's child seeks refuge with his mother's brother or other members of mother's patrilineage in case of a dispute with his own agnates. Their requests that he be forgiven are likely to be met because of the tradition of courtesy and cooperation that prevails between affinal kinsmen.

The Mossi further rationalize the permissiveness in this relationship with mother's descent group by explaining that because a person is "not related" to her lineage he cannot "spoil" its name. Since there is no legal tie between them, they have no basis for selfish interest in the success of his endeavors or the consequences of his public comportment. Thus for the elder members of mother's patrilineage, at least, the expression of affection toward him is uninhibited by the concerns that often temper their tendencies to indulge their own younger kinsmen.

The ancestral spirits of mother's agnatic kin group share the permissive attitude of their living descendants toward a sister's son. Consequently a child can make sacrifices to them and ask for their assistance in his activities with the assurance of greater benevolence than he can anticipate from the ancestral spirits of his own agnatic kin group. As an adult, the greater permissiveness of a person's relations to the ancestral spirits of mother's patrilineage is utilized. He often acts as ceremonial intermediary between them and their own ancestral spirits. For the Mossi believe that if an offering is inadequate or in any other way displeasing the ancestral spirits will be more likely to forgive a sister's son than one of their own patrilineal descendants.

Because of the importance of this relation to mother's lineage, avunculocal residence is most important among the alternative patterns of residence that provide the Mossi social system with a useful additional source of flexibility. An adult Mossi usually takes up residence with his mother's patriclan for either of two reasons. If he has had a quarrel with the members of his own agnatic kin group and has sought refuge from their displeasure and punishment in the household of mother's brother, he often remains even after he marries. Avunculocal residence also occurs frequently among the younger sons in minor lineages for whom adequate farmland and living space within the patriclan may not be available. When this occurs, sister's son and his descendants remain under the formal authority of their own patriclan elder. Typically the economic and social interaction that follows from a man's residence with mother's patriclan is complemented by the important sacerdotal responsibilities he assumes there. As has been stated because of the extension of the greater permissiveness characteristic of his relation with mother's living patrilineage to her ancestral spirits, the actual sacrifices to the ancestral spirits are most often made by a sister's son.

A still further variant to the predominant pattern of patrilocal residence occurs when a childless man requests his mother's lineage to send him a child to raise. Such a young person, raised in the patriclan residence of his father's sister's husband, assumes the role of a male member of the lineage with rights to the use of land, to call on father's sister's sons and their kinsmen for assistance with his farm work, and to construct for himself a house contiguous to the walls of the patriclan residence.

The dominant pattern of residence among the Mossi and the

alternatives to it provide a guide to the manner in which the primacy of patrilineal descent and patrilocal residence are importantly complemented by the existence of a variety of alternatives. Each is provided by a different kin group with which a person possesses, or can establish, a basis for sustained economic and social interaction sanctioned and strengthened by one of the many ties of kinship. The result is a social system that, if its rules are observed, assures individual, group, and community security.

ASSOCIATIONS

Several associations serve to extend still further the diffused field of relationships upon which the Mossi can rely for support. Because they increase the chances of adjustment by providing a variety of alternative bases for interaction, they serve also to lend greater flexibility to Mossi society as a system. Some of them complement the kinship system by providing for analogous functions outside the individual's sphere of consanguineal and affinal ties. Others cut across kinship lines and serve indirectly to strengthen them.

The Bond-Friend

Among these relationships the one characterized by the most intense emotional and intellectual involvement is that of the bond-friend. The generic term for this relationship is *dao menga*, "my man." It is established between men of the same approximate age who are unrelated in the agnatic line. Although women also have bond-friends, the relationship has no special name, probably a manifestation of the fact that the lesser social and economic mobility of women makes reliance on any sort of associational tie necessarily less intense and sustained. As nonkinsmen, bond-friends are bound together only by amity and a constantly reinforced tradition of cooperation.

A Mossi often has several bond-friends ranked in terms of the relative frequency and intensity of contact. Such relationships usually develop out of childhood friendships that are strengthened by occasions to render mutual aid, which results in a reciprocal obligation for support that grows into a permanent alliance perpetuated by the ongoing exchange of goods and services. No ceremony is involved. The relationship is reinforced as it continues to serve the needs of the participants. One of its important economic functions relates to the problem of individual enterprise and private property which has already been discussed. Bond friends often serve as preferred partners in economic activities that involve market exchange—working together in the local market or going off together to sell their labor in the cities or on the plantations.

The relationship also has important social functions. The manner in which Mossi relationships are characterized by indirection in communication and social interraction makes the role of intermediary an important one. For example, the bond-friend is used to establish contact with a girl in whom one partner is interested sexually. His friend acts as go-between, and it is often he who delivers the gifts made to her and to her mother when his partner's intentions become more serious. In formal marriage arrangements as well, bond-friends assist one another in making visits to the girls' kinsmen and may even help raise money for the purchase of the required gifts. After marriage the bond-friend frequently assumes the role of confidant in discussing his partner's marital difficulties or his plans for taking an additional wife.

It was noted earlier that Mossi marriage relationships are characterized by minimal emotional and intellectual involvement between man and wife, and that the separation of the sexes in childhood and adolescence continues into adulthood and the marriage relationship where it is reinforced by separation in most economic, social, and ceremonial roles. This separation is still further strengthened by the persistence after marriage of the bond-friend relationship which continues to constitute for each marriage partner, but particularly for the husband, a source not only of social and economic support, but also of intellectual and emotional closeness.

The bond-friend relationship is also valuable to the respective agnatic kin groups of participants, for their cooperation and good will often form the basis of a similar bond of social and economic cooperation between their lineages. Frequently, for example, when a man is away on a trip his bond-friend takes his place in the patriclan, assisting with farm work or helping prepare for a ceremonial.

Because the amity that unites bond-friends extends to their

". . . bond-friends often serve as preferred partners in economic activities . . . going off together to sell their labor in the cities . . ."

respective agnatic kinsmen, such a kin group is regarded as a good place to seek a wife. For affiliation will be acquired with a lineage with which a formalized relationship of friendliness has already been established. Marriage most often develops out of the relation established between a man and the lineage of an elder brother's bond-friend. If such a young man is poor and unable to begin negotiations for a bride with the expected presents to her parents, he may request permission to perform premarital bride service. He requests farmland from the elder of his brother's bond-friend's lineage and works it as if he were a member of the lineage himself, assuming his share in the economic and social responsibilities that unite its members. If he proves to be a productive resident of the patriclan, he may then ask them for a girl to marry. And if he is given a wife, he may remain on for a period of years as a resident member of his wife's residential kin group. By this means relationships that began voluntarily as associations are frequently reinforced later by the establishment of affinal ties.

Age Grades

In addition to these personal ties that serve to unite individuals with others outside their kin groups and by extension often serve to unite their kinsmen as well, every Mossi is related to his peers throughout the community on the basis of membership in a common age set, *bakyeda tase.*

The Mossi age grade, *reemen tase,* is community wide and includes all persons of the same sex and relative age. The membership in each grade is comprised of a number of age sets each containing all members of a group who were initiated together at puberty. Such groups are not ranked but are organized by village sector. Leadership in the male age set is assumed by the first boy to be circumcised. In the female set it is ascribed to the first girl to undergo the clitoridectomy. Among children the leader of the age set organizes recreational activities for the group. If the set affiliates with another of opposite sex in order to form the work group described in the last chapter, it is the leader of the boys' age set who has final authority over the entire membership.

Although the Mossi age grade itself does not fulfill any corporate functions, its members are expected to cooperate with one another,

and joking is expected between them. Age-set and age-grade affiliation function most significantly as a basis for cohesion among
unmarried young people and as an important source of pressure for
conformity with the patterns of behavior regarded as appropriate
for persons of a particular age. Among older boys it provides the
basis for the organization of migrant laborers. Following marriage
the importance of the age set and age grade decrease as members'
responsibilities to their kin groups grow. For women, who marry
earlier than men and are often residentially separated from their
age-set mates, the cohesive bond of the group is loosened even
sooner.

Joking Alliances

The relationship between agnatic kin groups which is called
dykya, a term that means literally "to buy millet," is characterized
by an even stronger expectation of joking between participants.
The term for the relationship refers to a recurrent aspect of the
content of joking between the individuals and groups that share
this institutionalized tie—the jocular assertion that the others are
their slaves and can be sold in the market to purchase grain.
Lineages related in this manner are expected to joke with one
another without fear of causing offense. An account follows of the
way such a relationship between two kin groups was said to have
been established.

Two lineages arrived at Lago at the same time. The elder of one
group went to the chief to request permission to settle there. He
explained that he had some slaves with him, actually the members
of the other kin group who were accompanying him. The chief
granted them a place to construct their houses and gave them some
farmland. Later the members of the second lineage learned that the
elder of the first group had described them to the chief as slaves.
They were angry and denied that this was so, saying "If you can
say we are your slaves so easily when you know we are not, then
we can say the same of you! You are our slaves!"

Now because they live side by side, because there often persists
between them a potential for conflict over the boundaries of their
respective farmlands, and because there is the memory of this
deception between them, they must always laugh and joke with one

another. Neither must ever do anything to harm the other, and each is expected to render economic and social assistance, to cooperate when necessary with farm work, and to avoid competition with the opposite group in community affairs. Joking between members of the two groups can occur without distinctions of status or age. A small child, when he sees an elder member of the other lineage approach can, for example, call out, "Ha, today I have good luck; I didn't have any money and now here comes money walking toward me. Come, I'm going to take you to market and sell you," to which the elder responds, "Who says so? Before you were born I was making money selling your kinsmen. Come, let's go to market and see who sells whom." To this the child can reply "No, that's not necessary. I already have the money, I'll just give your name to my friend and he'll come and take you later." "You'd better take the money back," the elder replies, "because no one is going to buy me. If you don't want to return the money, go and give your old father to your friend. He's used to being sold as a slave!" This sort of exchange is always accompanied by much laughter and, often, by some mock physical aggression, as each seizes the other and pretends to try and carry him off to market.

The kin groups that share this relationship appear generally to hold vague and potentially conflicting rights to certain common land, and their compound residences are usually contiguous. Joking between them serves effectively to reduce the tension resulting from this persistent source of potential conflict by communicating in an acceptable manner their grievances and thus perpetuating indirectly the amity necessary to support the cooperation upon which they are both reliant.

Marriage to a person belonging to another kin group with which this alliance exists is regarded as being particularly favorable because there already exists between the two a tradition of cooperation and a culturally sanctioned channel for the expression of frustration. In such a marriage the respectful distance a young girl would otherwise be expected to maintain from her husband's kinsmen, especially his elders, is somewhat suspended. Just as all members of his lineage can joke with her openly, frequently referring to her as their slave, so can she answer by saying that she commands them, that "her father sent her to them to look out for his property." However such joking is only proper with the members of the two groups who are of approximately the same age. With her husband's parents a girl is still expected to show respect. And while her husband may relax somewhat the formalized comportment that would otherwise be mandatory in relations with his wife's parents, he also must show them respect.

Guests

A further important association among the Mossi serves to extend the network of cooperative relationship beyond the local community. This is the guest relationship, *ga soba*. The term means literally "sleep person" and refers to the hospitality and lodging that partners in this relationship extend to one another. Its function and the values attached to it by the Mossi are illustrated by the proverb that says "A well fed guest is the *ya soba* [member of mother's agnatic kinsman] of his host." This refers to the analogy between this relationship and the valued one that exists between a man and the members of his mother's patrilineage, and indicates that reciprocal generosity between guests and hosts can lead to the strengthening and perpetuation of a mutually rewarding alliance.

The relationship appears to have its origin in the development of a tie of mutual cooperation between individuals that is gradually diffused to include the kinsmen of each, much as the amity between bond-friends comes to be extended to their respective agnatic kin groups. The principal function of the guest relationship appears to be the provision of food, shelter, and support in a strange community. It is usually established only in those villages where a man has no close affinal or consanguineal ties. The local partner provides his associate from another village not only with shelter and food but often with an opportunity to learn about those aspects of the situation in the vicinity that may affect the success of his errand there. In matters of great importance involving, for example, communication with strangers of superior status, the lodger acts as intermediary.

There are no ceremonial observances marking either the establishment or the dissolution of the guest relationship. It appears to persist as long as it is mutually rewarding. As an alternative source of social support, its importance seems to be growing. The increased mobility of the Mossi manifested in the growing reliance on

individual economic endeavors such as migratory labor and market
exchange as a means of getting a living, combined with the desira-
bility of carrying on such transactions outside the context of the
lineage system, suggest that the guest relationship, like other Mossi
associations, will probably increase in importance.

First in the life of the individual and in the organization of the
Mossi community is the patriclan. Its component parts—the
elementary family, the polygynous household, and the extended
family—together comprise a corporate whole. Beyond the patriclan
are the neighboring compound residences of other lineages in the
sib. Beyond the sib each individual and each patriclan is tied to the
surrounding community by an intricate network of affinal ties. The
relation to mother's agnatic kin group is especially close. Community cohesion is further reinforced by the ties of bond friendship,
joking alliance, and membership in common age sets and grades.
Many kin ties extend beyond the local community. Where they do
not, the guest relationship fills the gap. The result of this interlocking complex of kinship relations and the overlay of associational
bonds is a social context sufficiently extensive and flexible to provide the Mossi individual with an enviable measure of security and
the community with stability and continuity.

The social organization of the Mossi derives its basic reason for
being from the integration that exists between the technology and
the natural milieu. The allocation of land, the organization of work,
and the system of distribution are provided by the social organization—principally the kinship system—in response to needs that
have their origins in this particular integration. So long as it persists,
the essential stability of the Mossi social system is assured. Once it
is altered, social change is soon likely to follow.[5]

5. I have dealt elsewhere with some aspects of the social conse-
quences of technological change among the Mossi (cf. Peter B.
Hammond, "Economic Change and Mossi Acculturation," in W. R.
Bascom and M. J. Herskovits (eds.), *Continuity and Change in African
Cultures,* Chicago: University of Chicago Press, 1959, pp. 238–56;
"Management in Economic Transition," in W. E. Moore and A.
Feldman (eds.), *Labor Commitment and Social Change in Developing
Areas,* New York: SSRC. 1960, pp. 109–22, and "The Niger Project:
Some Cultural Sources of Conflict," in W. H. Lewis (ed.), *Emerging
Africa,* Wash., D.C.: Public Affairs Press, 1963, pp. 12–28.

CHAPTER SIX

POLITICAL ORGANIZATION

Only the descendants of the Mossi invaders from the south have the right to hold political office in Yatenga. Conversely the right to assume the role of Earth priest has been retained as the special prerogative of the agnatic descendants of the indigenous inhabitants. The relationship is symbiotic. Each of the two principal groups in the population has responsibility for maintaining order within one of the two complementary dimensions of the Mossi milieu.

LIMITATIONS ON THE STRENGTH OF POLITICAL AUTHORITY

The political organization of the Mossi derives its structure and important aspects of its function from the kinship system. The organization of political authority, the sanctions upon it, and the processes of decision making are all almost wholly analogous to those that order relations between kinsmen. But, perhaps most importantly, it is the dominant role of the lineage system in regulating Mossi society which explains in large part why the political organization, despite its apparently centralized structure and somewhat impressive sumptuary accoutrements, is not more significant in the administration of community, intracommunity, tribal, and intratribal affairs. It appears that it is not more important for the simple reason that it does not need to be.

In partial support of this contention, and before the structure and function of the Mossi political system can be effectively described and assessed, the economic and social functions of the Mossi kinship system, detailed in the two preceeding chapters, should be briefly reviewed.

The manner in which most economic activities related to subsistence are directed by the eldest responsible male members of each of the productive units of the kin group—the nuclear and polygynous families, the extended family, the patriclan, and sib— has been described. This authority is adequate to the ordering of most day-to-day activities in the life of the individual, his kin group, and his community. The way in which the function of the lineage system as a source of societal order is lent flexibility by the complementary role of mother's agnatic kin group has also been indicated. The ultimate authority of the sib elder, which represents the widest extension of authority based on the principle of consanguinity, has similarly been identified; it is supported by his right to withdraw economic support, social recognition, and ritual protection. The Mossi who fails to accept his authority not only is threatened by the possibility of economic and social sanctions, but also risks so angering the ancestral spirits that they may cause him to fall ill or his crops to fail.

It has been suggested that sib exogamy, the prohibition against marriage with a member of mother's lineage, and the preferred observance of village endogamy serve to extend still further the bonds of kinship as a basis for community cohesion, cooperation, and conflict control. Finally marriage between the members of spatially contiguous lineages located on the borders between Mossi villages extends the principle of kinship even more to provide a basis for intercommunity amity as well. This is complemented by the marriage of village chiefs and their close agnates with members of noble lineages—particularly the lineages of chiefs, located in neighboring communities.

The role of Mossi associations in complementing and crosscutting kinship relations to provide the individual and the group with a variety of alternative sources of social and economic support, and a series of alternative bases for the regulation of conflict, has also been described.

With regard to Mossi religion, a subject taken up in the next chapter, that aspect of the religious system that concerns the regulation of man's relationship to the various sources of supernatural power upon which he depends for economic and social security provides a still further important source of conservatism and control. The fear of angering the Earth deity and so risking withdrawal of the supernatural sources of earth fertility and of angering the deity that sends the rains or other deities that might send sickness to the farmer or to his helpers or sickness to his crops themselves, all illustrate the point. The common set of religious beliefs shared by members of the essentially autonomous Mossi community serve as a significant source of societal stability, cohesion, and order.

Beyond kinship and religion there exist still other nonpolitical mechanisms for the maintenance of order in Mossi society. Most important among them is the conservative function of social pressure. The village community is small and all its members know one another. Privacy is nearly impossible. Literally almost anything a Mossi does is done in the presence of others.

Even a slight deviation from the accustomed, traditionally sanctioned manner of behaving is likely to be perceived immediately. If it represents a potentially threatening digression from the established code of conduct, it is quickly met with ridicule. Songs and poems are composed and sung or recited at the market and at social dances concerning anyone who behaves unconventionally. Taken up by children and by age mates, the life of the subject is soon made miserable. Like most people the Mossi do not enjoy being laughed at, and they quickly abandon behavior that brings such derision. Given the near impossibility of achieving even temporary anonymity in Mossi society, such pressures function importantly as sources of social control.

Thus, among those individuals and groups most involved in sustained economic and social interaction there exists both a reason and a variety of means for maintaining order. Interdependence—technological, economic, social, supernatural, and emotional—is the

reason. And kinship relations, associations, and religious beliefs
and rituals provide the means. In short, most problems related to
the maintenance of social cohesion among the Mossi can be dealt
with without recourse to the political system.

A brief examination of Mossi torts and the manner in which they
are detected, adjudicated, and settled will further substantiate this
contention. Murder, incest, theft, sorcery, and adultery, more or
less in that order, are the crimes the Mossi regard as most serious.

Murder within the lineage is defined as fratricide and is punished
by death. Judgment is passed by the elders under the authority of
the sib headman. The accused is given a hearing and may call
witnesses. Any member of the kin group may also testify, either
in support of the accused or his accuser. If convicted, the person is
either flogged to death or strangled. Imposition of the death
sentence also serves as a means of ritual expiation, for the
ancestral spirits demand the death penalty and would punish the
elders and other members of the lineage if it were not carried out.'

Murder between affinally related persons is adjudicated by the
elders of their respective lineages according to the same process.
But in addition to the imposition of the death penalty, a fine to be
paid in cattle, sheep, grain, and money is imposed upon the lineage
of the murderer by his victim's kin group.

Murder of a nonkinsman who is a resident of the same ritual area
is adjudicated by the Earth priest according to essentially the
same process. The accused and his accusers may each call witnesses.
Two forms of divination and ordeal may also be used by the Earth
priest to determine guilt. If he claims to be innocent, the accused
may offer a white sheep or a chicken to the Earth deity as proof of

1. Technically, responsibility for dealing with such crimes passed
to the European administration during the French colonial period and
is now the charge of the newly established judicial system of the Voltaic
Republic. In fact such crimes occur rarely. However, when they do
occur, there is a question as to the percentage of such cases that are
actually reported to the "modern" authorities. During the French
regime word on such matters, especially in the rural areas, could only
get to the French administrator through his interpreter, an office that
proved to be powerful. The specifics of the interpreter's relations with
potential litigants—especially with regard to their generosity to him—
had an important effect on whether the need for legal action was ever
made known to the European administrator.

his innocence. The way the animal falls when it is killed, as this is determined by the Earth deity, will reveal guilt or innocence. If the defendant is guilty he must then be killed. And those of his kinsmen who have supported his plea of innocence must present "dark animals," symbols of guilt, in expiation. Otherwise the anger of the Earth deity will extend to them as well. The accused may also seek to prove his innocence by drinking water that has been poured over the Earth shrines. If he is guilty, the Earth deity will poison him with this water. If he is innocent he will be unharmed.

Thus in the instance of murder within the lineage system, within the context of affinal relationships, or among co-residents of a single ritual area—in other words, among groups most likely to come into conflict serious enough to result in murder, over land, property, or women—a means of settlement and the restoration of societal and supernatural harmony is provided outside the context of the political system.

Only murder involving nonrelated persons within the local community is adjudicated and settled by the village chief in consultation with his council of elders. The process is otherwise analogous to the one just described.

Incest is, of course, a crime that can only occur within the kin group, and it is settled there by the confiscation of the property of the participants and their banishment. This punishment also serves as expiation. It is demanded by the ancestors who, if it were not invoked, would punish the entire lineage.

Theft among the Mossi most often involves grain. Otherwise there is not much to steal; individuals have little portable private property of negotiable value. What they have—animals, clothing, and objects of European origin such as bicycles, lanterns, and flashlights—is readily identifiable, especially as those most likely to have access to such property are fellow agnates and co-residents of the patriclan who could be quickly detected. In contrast, the possession of stolen grain is difficult to prove. The thief must be caught in the act. Millet is usually stolen just before the harvest, cut from the stalk and surreptitiously stored away in the thief's granary. If grain is stolen by a kinsman, despite the charms used to protect the fields and the owners surveillance, which is likely to be especially keen just before the harvest, the crime is judged by the lineage elders, again, with accuser and accused permitted to call witnesses. A convicted person is flogged and fined. An incorrigible or inveterate thief may be expelled from the lineage.

Theft among affines or among the inhabitants of a ritual area is dealt with either by the elders of the kin groups involved or by the local Earth priest. Thus, once again, among those groups most likely to steal from one another—kinsmen working contiguous fields, affines, or others living in the same ritual area—there exists a means of dealing with such a delict without recourse to the political system. Only theft between nonkinsmen and those living at some distance from one another would require the intervention of the chief. But such thefts rarely occur because such persons do not have access either to the residence or to the farmlands of otherwise potential victims. To enter the house of a stranger undetected would be nearly impossible because of the compound structure of the Mossi dwelling. To enter a field far from one's own farmlands would be equally risky.

Sorcery is controlled in the same manner. Most accusations of sorcery occur among affines, either among co-wives or between a woman and the members of her husband's lineage. Such accusations are settled by the lineage elders.

Adultery is also dealt with within the family. An adulterous woman caught by her husband may be divorced or merely beaten by him. Given the absence of profound emotional attachment between Mossi husbands and wives, such a beating is often regarded as sufficient, and less bother, than a divorce. The wives of her partner may beat her if she is caught in their husband's house. She may also be subjected to painful public ridicule. Formerly chiefs' wives were put to death for adultery, as were their partners. Now they are emprisoned. Otherwise a man who commits adultery is subject only to being publicly ridiculed by his wife or wives, or, occasionally, to a beating at the hands of the kinsmen of his partner's husband.

These are the principal crimes committed in Mossi society. All of them can almost always be dealt with outside the political system.

Thus both in the regulation of daily activities in the local community and in the control and settlement of conflict among its members, the kinship system, complemented and reinforced by ritual sanctions, largely provides for the maintenance of societal order. Consequently it is suggested the political organization in Yatenga is weak for good reason. Because it does not have very much to do in the maintenance of internal order in the local community, in the regulation of relations between communities, or, since the colonially imposed abolition of intertribal warfare, in the conduct of affairs between the Mossi and their neighbors.

This contention provides a necessary preface to the following effort to assess realistically the structure and function of the units that comprise the Mossi political system.

THE VILLAGE, TENGA

Villages in Yatenga are organized into sectors, each of which is comprised of a cluster of patriclan compound dwellings housing the majority of localized lineages of the sib. Within each of the component patriclan residences it is the eldest responsible male who has authority. And it is the elder of the founding lineage of the sib whose authority is final within the sector. These sib elders serve also as counselors to the village chief, *Tenga Naba*, who is also an elder in the lineage system, the eldest responsible male member of the founding lineage of his own agnatic kin group.

Consequently the entire local political organization derives its structure from the kinship system. The supernatural sanctions on authority are similarly derived. Just as the authority of the village elders is supported by their close relation to the powerful spirits of their ancestors, so is the village chief, as eldest male member of the founding lineage of his sib, closest to the spirits of the former chiefs and, within his own kin group, the person who is formally responsible for their ritual propitiation. The closeness of his relation to his ancestors has two important consequences. He is able to invoke their punishment upon those who fail to accept his authority and, equally important, he himself is liable to supernatural punishment if he does not fulfill his political functions properly— that is, if he fails to act in accordance with the canons of proper chiftainship which his ancestors established.

The right to chiefly office at the village level is the prerogative of certain kin groups referred to collectively as *nakomse*—those with the right to rule. Some chiefs are elders of minimal lineages of the Yatenga Naba's own sib, a group referred to collectively as *reem namba,* a term that means, literally, "those who impose themselves upon us." Only the chief himself, his wives, and his own immediate descendants enjoy any significantly superior social status in the local community. The majority of the members of a chiefly lineage have an economic and social position that is in no way different from that of other Mossi villagers. They are farmers, like all the Mossi, and neither they themselves, nor their wives or children have any special prerogatives or privileges.

The land holdings of a chief are typically more extensive than those of other Mossi farmers, and they are worked by his more extended household. Chiefs have many wives, from ten to thirty-five or forty, depending on their wealth and the importance of their village. These women are taken from most of the principal lineages of the village and from kin groups, often chiefly lineages, in neighboring villages. This makes the chief an affinal kinsman of nearly every local lineage but his own and establishes a basis for amicable interaction with neighboring communities as well; another instance in which kinship permeates the political system.

As was stated, the chief's farmlands are worked not only by his own kinsmen, but also by representatives of all sectors of the village. And after the harvest he is paid further tribute. These contributions are regarded by the Mossi as payment for services rendered. For the chief has the responsibility of assuring the maintenance of the societal stability and peace essential to the operation of their technology and the conduct of the economic and social activities necessary to their subsistence and well-being. The relationship is redistributive. They give him labor and farm produce in return for the assurance of social order and the protection of his ancestral spirits. Such economic support is due the chief so long as he meets his responsibilities in maintaining the well-being of the community.

It is only when conflict cannot be resolved within the lineage or within the larger network of affinal, ritual, or associational ties, that recourse to the political system is taken. The chief can enforce the banishment or order the beating of a person convicted of a crime. But such a decision is made only after the plaintiff and the accused have both been heard. However, in accordance with the strong reliance on indirection characteristic of Mossi social interaction involving important issues, verbal confrontation between the principals themselves, and between either of the principals and the

"Only the chief himself, his wives, and his own immediate descendants enjoy any significantly superior social status."

chief, is frequently avoided. Elders within the respective descent groups of the litigants, their mother's brothers, or bond-friends serve most often as intermediaries.

But such conflict occurs infrequently. Strangers in a Mossi village are rare. If they are present in a community, it is usually because of a kinship tie of one sort or another. If they are merely passing through, there is little reason that they should come into such violent conflict with a local inhabitant that blood would flow and the chief's intervention be made necessary.

The daily round of Mossi activities and the life experience of most individuals involve sustained interaction only with persons with whom they share one or more common bonds of relationship. Consequently it is only in a community far distant from their own, or actually lying beyond the frontiers of Yatenga, that they would be likely to come into contact with persons with whom conflict might result in overt expressions of hostility and physical violence. But the kin group, the patriclan, and the local community are so autonomous and provide so well for their members' economic and social needs that such contact, and the resultant possibility of conflict, are unlikely to occur.

In brief, where control of conflict and its resolution is necessary, it exists in Mossi society. Where the potential for conflict is minimal, the possibilities of controlling its development are minimal also.[2]

Fighting does, of course, occur among Mossi villagers, but it is infrequent and is almost always quickly brought to an end. It occurs most often among young men as the result of quarrels over girls. While it is expected that a man who has been insulted or otherwise seriously angered in such a dispute should show great rage and attempt to do his antagonist harm, it is also expected that his kinsmen and close friends will restrain him. If there is no bloodshed, and there rarely is, the quarrel is likely to be quickly settled by the principals being forced apart. If the source of their conflict involves the interests of their lineages, informal talks will take place

2.   This is generally true of societies organized on the basis of lineage segmentation and fission. Spatial contiguity and closeness of relationship are positively correlated. And, conversely, the degree of spatial separation tends to be complemented by a parallel degree of genealogical distance.

between their respective headmen and an effort will be made to settle the matter there. If this is not possible, the dispute may be taken to the chief for a hearing and judgment.

It is only when fighting occurs among individuals or groups who share no institutionalized basis for the re-establishment of amity that hostility may be perpetuated unless the chief intervenes. When this is necessary, representatives from both sides are heard and anyone else involved may also speak. After such a hearing a judgment is made by the chief in consultation with his counselors, the elders of the village kin groups. The pattern for the entire procedure is established by custom. Its observance is jealously guarded by the ancestors of the chief and all those who advise him. A decision that violates tradition may result in supernatural punishment of the entire community.

The second dimension of the chief's political role, that which involves his responsibility for the maintenance of order in relations between his village and neighboring communities, is similarly limited. Here again, it is impossible to ignore the role of kinship, for through marriage, the chief, his kinsmen, and many of his fellow villagers are likely to share affinal and consanguineal ties with kin groups residing in most nearby villages. Among such kinsmen, particularly affines, the requirements for cooperation and friendliness between in-laws, the control of conflict through institutionalized joking between siblings-in-law, and the self-interest of each group in maintaining amicable ties provide sources for cooperation and the control of conflict that serve to extend in a significant manner the basis of amity and stability beyond the limits of the local community.

Many Mossi villages share an institutionalized joking relationship with their neighbors. Typically, it is their respective chiefs who, when they come into contact with one another, are expected to joke in the humorous but hostile manner that is always characteristic of this relationship in Mossi society. As is the case in institutionalized joking between lineages, this is accompanied by an expectation of cooperation. Here, as wherever such joking occurs among the Mossi, it seems to be present when there exists between two or more groups both the potential for conflict over rights to land or hunting territory, and the requirement to cooperate, a manifestation of their mutual recognition of the dangers of overt hostility in the relations between contiguous communities.

Farming their respective lands would obviously be made difficult and hazardous unless there existed between neighboring villages a minimal degree of friendliness. Where such a joking relationship is present, conflicts over land claims, although they may involve real differences of opinion as to respective rights, can never develop into disputes. The joking relationship does not allow for this. It is expected that whenever inhabitants from either village meet one another they should joke, and that their chiefs should also joke. This expectation provides, immediately that such individuals come into conflict, a means of expressing without fear of offense or retaliation the exact nature of their grievance. This, in turn, provides a permissive context for discussion which allows all parties involved to rectify whatever behavior is seriously threatening the perpetuation of amity in their relations.

In those rare instances in which it is impossible to regulate conflict by these indirect means—by reliance on a kinship tie, shared membership in a single ritual area, or the joking relationship—recourse must first of all be taken to conciliation between the chiefs involved. If they, in consultation with their respective village counselors, are unable to arrive at a settlement of the dispute, it must then be taken to the canton chief for adjudication.

THE CANTON

Most Mossi villages are organized into cantons under the authority of a chief who is often a member of the Yatenga Naba's own descent group. The canton chiefs receive tribute from the villages under their jurisdiction and, in turn, are expected to maintain social order and, through ritual intercession with the spirits of their ancestors, a benevolent relation to the supernatural. In addition to their only occasionally necessary role in the settlement of disputes between villages, they act as intermediaries between the villagers under their control and the still more important, if not necessarily more powerful, provincial chiefs.

They serve also as links in the redistributive system which maintains the Mossi political organization. Like village chiefs who receive tribute from the villagers, the canton chiefs receive tribute from the chiefs subordinate to them, and, in turn, must pass on a portion to their superiors, the provincial chiefs.

The status of Mossi canton chiefs is reflective of a principle basic to the structure and function of the entire political hierarchy in Yatenga. The "higher" the office and the more elaborate its sumptuary and ritual accoutrements the less is its real power. It appears likely that the role of canton chief was more important prior to the colonially imposed intertribal and intratribal peace. For then the canton chiefs, like their subordinates the village chiefs, and their superiors, the provincial chiefs, had a more important function to fulfill—mobilization for offense and defense, transmission of directives from the king, and supervision of the redistribution of war booty. But those days are past.

THE PROVINCE, SOLUM

The cantons of Yatenga are further organized into a number of provinces, *solumse,* or "commands," each of which is governed by a chief who serves also as one of the principal ministers to the king, the Yatenga Naba.

Like the village chiefs, the right of provincial chiefs to political office is determined by their position within the kinship system. That is, as senior male members of the founding lineage of a noble sib which has the right to the chieftainship at the provincial level, or as junior members of the royal sib.[3]

Provincial chiefs are rarely kinsmen of the Yatenga Naba. Although their political office and the functions connected with it resemble those of the Mossi village and canton chiefs, it is nonetheless distinctive in a number of ways. They are both more and less

3. I use the terms noble and royal because I am unable to find any other single terms that are more appropriate. But the translation in both instances must be understood to be loose; those whom I call "nobles" are the *nakomse,* a term that translates more or less literally as the descendants of the chief. The term I translate as *reemnamba* (or *deemdemba*) means "those who maintain themselves upon us," and is used to refer to the Yatenga Naba and the members of his lineage. However these usages are not to be understood as indications that Mossi society is stratified. It is only those members of such lineages who actually hold political positions, and their close agnates, who enjoy any significantly superior social status.

powerful. On the one hand they possess the authority to command the following of all chiefs residing within their province. In fact they rarely have occasion to do so, because no sort of action is coordinated at the provincial level. The only significant direction that takes place there involves the transmission of tribute from the villages to the king's court at Ouahigouya.

Provincial chiefs also serve as spokesmen for the Yatenga Naba. They have the responsibility of relaying his orders to the canton and village chiefs of their province. But, again, Mossi society is so organized by tradition and so sustained by the continuity of the technology and the largely autonomous lineage-based socioeconomic system that, in times of peace, there are few important directives to transmit. Most communications have to do with the regulation of ceremonial affairs, such as the announcement of the first festivals that mark the beginning of the ritual cycle that concludes the agricultural year and requires the presence in the capital of all important political figures.

The political boundaries of a particular Mossi province are not solely determined by geography. While their organization typically corresponds to a delimited area and comprises a cluster of cantons, the fact of authority over a particular category of the population is also critical. Thus one provincial chief and minister, the Baloum Naba, for example, has direct control over the southern regions of Yatenga and indirect control over Riziam and Zittenga, two cantons which never came to fully accept the central control of the Yatenga Naba. This same minister is also charged with maintaining liaison with the principal Earth priests throughout Yatenga. And he is administrator of one of the sectors of the capital city and acts there as a member of the Yatenga Naba's council. He carries on these diffuse administrative functions from his residence in Ouahigouya.

The political duties of the provincial chiefs are balanced in a significant manner. On the one hand they represent the ultimate source of provincial authority and are thus potentially able to command the following of the canton and village chiefs; they also have an adjudicative function within the province over which they have command; and they serve as spokesmen for the canton and village chiefs of their province in their dealings with the Yatenga Naba. These provincial political responsibilities are counterbalanced by their duties at the court in Ouahigouya. Their required presence there, and the expectation that they should reside in the capital itself, provide an effective means of controlling the concentration of political power at the provincial level, a development which might be potentially subversive to the successful maintenance of the centralized authority of the king.

The fact that provincial chiefs are not recruited from the sib of the Yatenga Naba is also significant in this regard. They can, as a consequence, act to impede the political ambitions of their subordinates, the canton chiefs, who often are members of the royal sib. For these several reasons Mossi provincial chiefs are more important as intermediaries in the political system than as sources of significant political power.

Just as the canton chiefs are in part supported by tribute from the villagers under their command, it is their responsibility to pass on a portion of the goods they receive to the provincial chief. Here again, the relation is perceived as redistributive. The canton chiefs recognize the authority of the provincial chief and pay him tribute in order to maintain a benevolent relationship to him and to assure that he will act as their sympathetic intermediary with the Yatenga Naba. The residence maintained by each provincial chief at Ouahigouya serves as a gathering place for villagers and village and canton chiefs alike when they have occasion to visit the capital. And if they seek favor with the Yatenga Naba, it is the responsibility of their provincial chief to represent them.

In addition to the Baloum Naba, the roles of a number of other provincial chiefs are important in the working of the Mossi political system. The Widi Naba, for example, presides over another sector of the capital, and has authority over those villages throughout Yatenga—regardless of their location—that are ruled not by the eldest member of a local chiefly sib, but by members of the Yatenga Naba's own descent group. Widi Naba is also charged with maintaining liaison between the king and the seminomadic Fulani of Yatenga.

Rassam Naba represents the interests of the smiths and all former slaves wherever they live in Yatenga. He is the Yatenga Naba's executioner and chief of protocol as well. Togo Naba has authority over all other Mossi villages. He is also the king's principal spokesman and arbitrates the process of succession following the king's death, exercising political authority himself until a successor is selected, a decision made by the provincial chiefs assembled during the interregnum to consider the claims of the deceased king's close and competing agnates.

THE KINGDOM, YATENGA[4]

The kingdom is the largest and most all-inclusive unit in the political organization of the Mossi. Its cultural role appears, superficially, to be somewhat paradoxical. For it represents the most extended dimension of political authority, and yet it is actually the least important locus for making those decisions that are critical to the maintenance of internal order and the regulation of external relations. The limited political significance of the Mossi kingdom is a further and final manifestation of a principle which has already been mentioned as basic to the function of the political process among the Mossi within every structural unit beyond the lineage and patriclan, from the sib through the village and canton to the province and kingdom: the positive correlation between the extensiveness of authority and its weakness.

The Mossi king is not so much to be perceived as placed at the apex of a pyramidal political structure, as at the symbolic center of a system more accurately described as a slightly asymmetrical, loosely woven web.

The Yatenga Naba is believed to be the direct descendant of Naba Yadega, the founder of Yatenga as a distinct political entity among the Mossi kingdoms. He also is supported by the receipt of a portion of the harvests taken from the villages. This tribute is relayed to him by the canton and provincial chiefs in recognition of the submission of the populations they represent to his authority and of their reliance on him for the maintenance of the social peace necessary to carry on their economic and social endeavors. The ceremonial context in which this occurs is described in Chapter 8.

On the occasion of these important political and religious ceremonials, the Yatenga Naba uses a part of the tribute he has received to prepare a sacrificial libation to the spirits of his predecessors in

4. Literally Yatenga means the country of Yadega, the first ruler. It does not mean kingdom and it does not mean that Yatenga fits the medieval European model with which the generic term "kingdom" is too often carelessly identified.

order to assure their continued benevolence toward him and his subjects, a benevolence necessary to assure the health and well-being of the Mossi population and the good weather necessary for the success of the crops. Thus on the state level as well, the redistributive principle operates. The Mossi render to the king a portion of their goods in order to maintain him and his household. In turn they anticipate that he will maintain the social order necessary to the conduct of their work.

Here also the system of ancestor worship functions to reinforce the system of political authority. For the spirits of the deceased kings are most powerful of all. Like the lesser spirits of the deceased provincial, canton, and village chiefs and the departed souls of former sib and lineage headmen, the spirits of the former Nabas of Yatenga can affect the well-being of the entire living population by withholding rains necessary for the crops, or by sending disease which might decimate the work force or cripple it seriously during important phases of the farming cycle.

Also, in a symbolic sense, all the inhabitants of Yatenga are the children of Naba Yadega, the first king, and are thus related to his successors in office.[5] If they behave according to the requirements of tradition, if they are obedient to the local chiefs and the king, they can expect that the spirits of the former Nabas of Yatenga will watch over them. Conversely, if they violate custom or disobey the authority of their elders, the chiefs, or the Yatenga Naba, they risk serious punishment: disease, death, and the possible destruction of their families, animals, and farms.

At every level in the political system those who hold office are referred to by kinship terms, either directly or indirectly. A village, canton, or provincial chief or the Yatenga Naba himself—or any close kinsman of these powerful figures—may be referred to as a senior kinsman, usually as *baba,* "father." The difference in relative position between subordinates and superiors in the political system

---

5. This represents a logical further extension of a system of thought about social relations that derives from participating in the Mossi kinship system. It results from the inevitable blurring of remote genealogical ties, the Mossi tendency to affiliate nonagnates through marriage, and interpretation of the political dependency of nonrelated peoples as analogous to the subordination of minor lineages within the sib.

is perceived as analogous to the difference in relative status and authority between a junior and a senior member of the kin group. The village chief is the father of all the villagers; the Yatenga Naba is the father of all the Mossi in Yatenga.

This perception of shared descent as basic to the structure of the political system represents an extension of a familiar aspect of contemporary reality. For the persistent fission of lineage segments results in the emergence of new kin groups, usually new lineages within the sib, which contain in small scale nearly all the basic features of the organization of the entire Mossi political system. They comprise a new group branched off from an older one, moving into new territory and establishing for themselves a partially distinctive economic, social, political, and ritual identity. Each time such fission occurs, the events that characterized the establishment of Yatenga as a separate political entity are reproduced in microcosm.

Thus the sense of common identity shared by the Mossi of Yatenga appears to be derived not from a sense of participating in a single political system, but of being the members of a single descent group. It is as children—or, in the instance of the indigenous inhabitants, as sister's sons—of Naba Yadega that they perceive their relation to one another, not as citizens of Yatenga. Their perception of their cultural affinities with the peoples of Ouagadougou and the other Mossi "kingdoms" takes a similar form. Their relations are regarded—probably correctly—as the consequence of an analogous but even more remote genealogical tie.

The threat of punishment by the ancestral spirits of the dead chiefs serves not only to control the behavior of the Mossi population at large, but also as an important source of conservatism in the deportment of the political leaders themselves. For just as their ancestral spirits may punish their subjects if they fail to conform to the canons of traditional behavior, so is a village canton, or provincial chief—or even the Yatenga Naba—who violates the requirements of customary political action likely to be punished by the spirits of his own powerful ancestors.

Consequently Mossi political leaders must always rely on established custom for guidance in making administrative decisions. The traditions of proper comportment that serve as guides to political action in the present are kept alive in the oral traditions and in the recollection of the elders. In making decisions every political leader

". . . the people support the chief in return for his successful
supervision of the maintenance of community order."

is expected to refer to the record of political action of his deceased kinsmen. This orally-maintained tradition constitutes an important aspect of Mossi law and serves as a significant source of conservatism not only in the political system but throughout Mossi culture.

In its traditional form the political system of the Mossi is well balanced. The organization and implementation of political action follows smoothly from the structure and processual principles that underlie the kinship system. Everything is in equilibrium. At the village level the people support the chief in return for his successful supervision of the maintenance of community order. If they fail to meet their responsibility to him, they risk the withdrawal of his support and the punishment of his ancestral spirits. Similarly if he fails to meet his responsibility to them he risks the withdrawal of their support, as well as the punishment of his ancestors' spirits. The same controls operate at the level of the canton, the province, and the kingdom.

Despite the superficial appearance of structural complexity, the Mossi political system is really peripheral to the processes by which social order is maintained in Yatenga. Relations within and between communities can usually be regulated on the basis of kinship, associational, or ritual ties.

And, as was previously suggested, the reasons for the primacy of such relationships are essentially technological. To a large extent the patriclan is technologically self-sufficient. The local community is almost entirely so. Within it the political system has only a small part to play. Internal order and the regulation of relations with neighboring patriclans and the village at large are taken care of by the lineage system and the complementary system of affinal ties. Associations, ritual ties, custom, and occasional social pressure do the rest. The entire pattern of social interaction was established by the ancestral spirits and is sanctioned by them.

Thus political centralization is really not now very critical to the maintenance of internal order in Mossi society. It may have been in the past—during the period of rapid political expansion that led to the establishment of the Yatenga dynasty, and during the period that followed in which reliance on pillage and tribute may have continued to constitute a significant source of material support for the king and his followers.

Warfare and cultural heterogeneity were, perhaps, linked characteristics in the political history of the Yatenga. Both are factors that may have contributed importantly to the perpetuation of centralized political authority once the Mossi had entered Yatenga, despite the fact that soon thereafter they ceased to rely on warfare as a means of maintaining or extending their political frontiers.

For not only did the Mossi settle among an autocthonous population whose cultural traditions were considerably different from their own, but there were also present in Yatenga minorities of Fulani and Mende origin. Thus at the outset there existed a population that was culturally heterogeneous. Even after the initial conquest need for centralized authority may, for a time, have continued to be necessary to adjust and regulate the technological, economic, and social interaction of these several ethnically distinct groups that now composed the Yatenga population. The Fulani and the Yarse of Yatenga have always occupied specialized roles within the context of Mossi society. The former as herdsmen to the settled Mossi farmers. And the latter as specialists in the market. Centralized administration may have been necessary because relations between these diverse groups could not be ordered on the basis of kinship, associational, or ritual ties. For at the outset there existed among them no bonds of common descent, shared tradition, or commonly held religious beliefs.

However the role of cultural heterogeneity in creating and perpetuating the need for political centralization among the Mossi is less than certain. For among other peoples of the Western Sudan, the Tallensi and Gourounsi, for example, this same cultural heterogeneity did not result in the development of strongly centralized political systems.

Warfare precipitated by population growth that was exceeding technological advancement persists as the apparently more important factor in explaining the development and perpetuation of centralized political authority among the Mossi. But there are problems with this explanation as well. For the process of lineage segmentation and fission as a response to growing population and shrinking land resources does not require political centralization or warfare for the accomplishment of territorial expansion.[6]

6. The work of Evans-Pritchard among the Nuer (*The Nuer*, Oxford: Clarendon Press, 1940) first demonstrated this. It has been

Whatever the historical factors that may have contributed to the development of a measure of political centralization among the Mossi—and it is, quite simply, beyond the intended scope of this book to enquire into them further—it appears that the imposition of indirect rule at the time of the French conquest was importantly related to the perpetuation of such centralization. At the same time the traditional functions associated with political status were systematically subverted. Only the village chiefs retained any measure of effective authority. The king and the provincial and canton chiefs became civil servants, dependent upon the French administration for their support and thus subject to its authority.

Thereafter the continued maintenance of the forms of the traditional centralized political system had scarcely any political significance. Neither canton chiefs, provincial chiefs, nor the Yatenga Naba made decisions necessary to the maintenance of internal social order. And in 1897 the incorporation of Yatenga into the cluster of colonies that was to become French West Africa obviated the problem of regulating external relations.

Whatever its previous functions, once the French conquest had been achieved the centralized political system of the Mossi could have been allowed to disintegrate gradually without any serious consequences for the continuity of the basic aspects of Mossi culture—their technology, economic organization, social system, or their religion. The validity of this contention is supported by events in Yatenga since the Upper Volta received its independence in 1960: The authority of traditional political leaders has declined steadily as a new national government has emerged.[7]

further substantiated in the works of Meyer Fortes, *The Dynamics of Clanship Among the Tallensi,* London: Oxford University Press for the International African Institute, 1945; Marshall Salsins, "The Segmentary Lineage: An Organization for Predatory Expansion," *American Anthropologist,* Vol. 63 (1961), pp. 322–45, and reprinted in Peter B. Hammond (ed.), *Cultural and Social Anthropology,* New York: Macmillan, 1964, pp. 181–200; Marshall Sahlins and Elman R. Service (eds.), *Evolution and Culture,* Ann Arbor: University of Michigan Press, 1960.

7. For a good account of this process see Skinner (1964).

CHAPTER SEVEN

RELIGION

The belief system of the Mossi, their perception of the supernatural and of their relation to it, and the observances that follow from this perception complete the orderly arrangement of their world. Just as they understand the structure and function of the technological, economic, social, and political dimensions of their milieu and know what actions are appropriate to perpetuate the security of their status within it, so do they have an equally orderly, and complementary, perception of their supernatural environment.

They believe that all aspects of this environment were created by the supreme being, *Wende,* and are animated by his force, *nam.* Thus the distinction between nature and the supernatural is hard to make. Implicitly every aspect of their natural environment, but especially those aspects that are related importantly to their technology, are vitalized by supernatural powers. The quality of these powers is understood and the actions necessary to control them are clearly comprehended. Not that the Mossi are always

successful in their efforts at control. They are not. But when they
fail they understand the reasons for that also. Supernatural power
is usually refered to as *Wennam*, "God's force." The specific
manifestations of the power of Wende are referred to as *Wende*
preceeded by the term for the particular aspect of the environment
with which they are identified. Thus, for example, *Tenga* (earth)
Wende is the earthly manifestation of the deity; but this does not
mean that Tenga Wende is a wholly distinct being.[1]

Life itself is an expression of the force of God. The souls of the
dead, the elements of nature, the efficacy of charms, and the power
of diviners all have their ultimate origin in Wende. The deity is
aloof from men. It is through his many specific manifestations that
he affects their lives, and it is toward these specific representations
of his force that human efforts to achieve security in relation to
the supernatural are directed.

Both Mossi cosmology and theology are localized and pragmatic;
they are concerned with the structure of the supernatural as it
affects the inhabitants of Yatenga. The Mossi accept unquestioningly
the nature of the supernatural order and are concerned only with
dealing with it efficiently. Generally they are not preoccupied with
speculation on theological or liturgical matters. What they know
of the nature of the supernatural they have learned from their
ancestors. What they have not learned they do not need to, and
cannot, know. No sanction in Mossi society is stronger than the
one that abjures them to follow in the *Rogo Miki*, the way of the
ancestors. In religion, as in most other aspects of life, tradition is
the most valued guide to action. This attitude, which is emphasized
throughout their educational system and affects all aspects of Mossi
life, discourages speculation as useless. The forces of the supernatural are as they are. The reason for worshipping them in a particular way is that it has always been done in that way. And that
is enough.

Analytically Mossi religious ideas and the actions that follow
from them can be divided into two principal categories—those that
explain and organize man's relation to nature, and those that sac-
tion the social order and provide guides to proper behavior within it.

1. In this the Mossi idea of God seems to differ from the concept
found elsewhere in West Africa of a creator deity surrounded by his
supernaturally less powerful progeny.

THE SUPERNATURAL FORCES OF NATURE

The natural manifestations of Wennam vitalize the Mossi milieu sanction the organization of the technology, and oversee its operation.

As the supernatural force that activates general climatic conditions and gives fertility to the soil, the deity is manifested as *Tenga Wende*, the Earth deity. As *Tido Wende*, the Plant deity, he is the source of plant growth. *Ki Wende*, the Millet deity, is the still more specific manifestation of the deity that is the source of life in the millet fields. *Saga Wende* is the aspect of the deity from which the rains come.

Maintenance of balance in relationship to these various natural manifestations of the deity is essential to the successful function of Mossi technology. The deity—in one or another of his forms—can give or take away the fertility of the fields, can withhold the vitality necessary for healthy plant growth and a rich harvest, and can grant or deny the abundant summer rains without which the crops would fail. He is generous and benevolent in his actions toward the Mossi so long as they observe his prohibitions and participate in the ceremonials designed to propitiate the various specific manifestations of his force.

These ceremonials mark each new phase in the advancing year: field preparation, planting, cultivation, the harvest and the festivals of thanksgiving that follow. The symbolic actions they entail tie men to one another and to the seasons, reifying the entire pattern of Mossi culture. Because of its close relation to the other aspects of Mossi culture, discussion of the ritual cycle will be reserved for the next chapter.

Most ritual prohibitions involving the natural manifestations of the deity relate to the sanctity of the earth. Tenga Wende, the Earth deity, is potentially responsive to any changes that occur on the land. All farmlands are under his ultimate control. This fact must be ritually acknowledged at the inception of each important phase in the process of land use or the undertaking will be likely to fail. The right to use land is also sanctioned by the ancestral spirits; but it is Tenga Wende who is the source of its supernatural properties. Unused land not owned by any kin group can only be cleared and put into cultivation after a sacrifice to the Earth deity has been made through the intercession of an Earth priest, *Tenga Soba*.[2] This must be renewed each year so long as the land is used. Failure to observe this ritual requirement is believed to anger the Earth deity and to result in a withdrawal of his force which will be manifested in the loss of soil fertility. Similarly, if a new well is to be dug, the Earth deity must first be notified. Otherwise the Mossi believe no water could be found.

Because all things on the land belong to the Earth deity, any unclaimed article of importance or value found there should be taken to the Earth shrine to be claimed by its owner or left to decompose gradually and return to the earth. Consequently the Mossi Earth shrines are often piled high with rusty knives, old hoe blades, bicycle parts, pieces of clothing, and disintegrating bits of basketry. As was previously indicated, outside the kin group theft within the ritual area under the control of a particular Earth priest is regarded as a violation of the sanctity of the Earth. For an object that has ceased to be under the proprietorship of an individual or his kin group reverts to the Earth deity. As is true with the operation of most forms of supernatural punishment among the Mossi, punitive action is not necessarily immediate. Rather, it is the thief's relation to the Earth which is damaged. This damage can be rectified by restitution of the stolen property and a sacrifice at the Earth shrine. Otherwise the displeasure of the deity is most likely to be manifested in withdrawal of the fertility of the thief's farmlands.

Sexual intercourse performed on the bare ground is also regarded as a defilement of the Earth. Intercourse should occur only on a mat, never on the ground itself and should take place only inside the house or in the courtyard. Failure to observe this prohibition also risks the withdrawal of soil fertility. Expiation for most violations of prohibitions related to the sanctity of the Earth requires a personal offering to the Earth deity. This usually takes the form of a chicken, and is accompanied by a request for pardon transmitted to the deity by the Earth priest.

2.   *Tenga*, in this instance means "earth." *Soba* means "person," in the sense of a person responsible for the Earth. As a one-word translation I prefer the term priest to the "custodian" used by Fortes and occasionally by Goody in their descriptions of these functionaries among the ethnically related Tallensi and Lo Willi.

". . . the Earth shrine . . ."

These Earth priests are the principal sacerdotal intermediaries between the Mossi and the natural manifestations of the deity. Although they are now called Mossi, they actually trace their descent from a people "indigenous" to Yatenga, the Nyonyose or Foulse, all of whose sibs are referred to as *Savadogo* which means, more or less literally, "descended from the rain clouds."[3] As a consequence of generations of lineage segmentation and fission, the descendants of these early Earth priests now belong to many, probably one hundred or more, separate sibs. It is the elders of the component patrilineages of these sibs who are the Mossi *Tenga Soba Namba,* the Earth priests.

According to the most usual version of their myth of origin, the first ancestor of the founding lineage of the Savadogo descended from the sky in a house without a door.[4] There was a noise inside. Those who heard it cut an opening and found there an Earth priest fully equipped with the accoutrements of his office: a tall red felt tarboosh, which in its present form appears to be of North African origin, a ceremonial hoe, *tenga soonga,* and the *tenga rakako,* a pronged staff about three feet in length, carried by the Earth priest on all ritual occasions. The ceremonial hoe has a shorter shaft, but is otherwise like the one used by the Mossi in cultivation. Although the spearlike *tenga racaco* is unlike the spears now used in the hunt, it may resemble a weapon used earlier and no longer manufactured because of the decreased importance of hunting. When a sacrifice is performed at the Earth shrine, these tools are crossed and laid over the altar so as to receive the offertory libations as they fall.

As pointed out, the boundaries of the ritual areas under the charge of the Earth priests do not correspond with the territorial limits of the villages, cantons, or provinces that are the units of political control. Often they cut across them. The farmlands within a single village frequently fall under the ritual authority of several different Earth priests. Even a single lineage may have farmlands that lie within several ritual areas. Conversely the elder of a single Savadogo lineage may be ritually responsible for an area encompas-

3. The Savadogo also call themselves Kouroumba or Kourou-mankobe, the term by which they are referred to in Tauxier (1917) and in the work of other early writers (cf. Vadier, *op. cit.* and Noire, *op. cit.*).

4. For another version of this myth see (Zahan, 1961, p. 13).

sing farmlands in several villages. The useful functions of this overlapping of religious and political jurisdictions have already been mentioned. It serves also as further evidence of the differing historical origins of these two complementary aspects of the Mossi's integrated system of social and supernatural controls.

Succession to the role of Earth priest follows the general Mossi pattern of descent and inheritance. At the death of a priest the position should be passed on to the next eldest male member of his generation within his minimal lineage. This occurs at the same time the heir assumes the role of sib elder. There is no formal ritual preparation for the assumption of this status. As with the learning of all techniques among the Mossi, preparation can only be accomplished by observation. A presumptive priest must learn his possible future role from observing the ritual actions of his elder kinsmen. If he is a member of the same patriclan, as should, of course, be the case, he often has an opportunity to assist the Earth priest and learns by participation the behavior that is appropriate to the office he will one day inherit. But this ritual assistance is not mandatory. If the compound residence of the Earth priest is isolated from the other lineage residences of the sib as a consequence of lineage segmentation, there is a problem—one that provides another example of the weakness of the Mossi educational system. For if the heir to the role of Earth priest is not a resident of the same household, opportunities for such observation may be limited; and if he has been unable to learn by observation, he cannot learn by asking questions or by formal training.

Consequently he very often succeeds to a ritual role with which he is only slightly familiar, often uncertain of the proper forms and, in some instances, wholly ignorant of the ideological rationale behind them. Other elder members of his lineage will assist him in mastering the simple ritual routines. And that, for the Mossi, is enough. No one will ask him to explain these rituals, and for those who are dependent on him for ritual intercession, it is sufficient to know that he is following the way of his ancestors.

If the deceased Earth priest's elder brother is unavailable to succeed him and he has no heirs, his ceremonial role can be assumed by a sister's son. Apparently this represents an extension to the Earth deity of the permissive relationship a person enjoys with the ancestral spirits of mother's patrilineage. And it is another example of the function of the residual reliance on uterine ties generally characteristic of the Mossi kinship system. Here also the relationship can be relied on to assure the indulgence of the Earth deity in overlooking the irregularity of the succession. The natural manifestations of the deity apparently enjoy with the priest's sister's son the same permissive and indulgent relationship that characterizes his relation to those other supernatural beings, the ancestral spirits of mother's patrilineage.

The Mossi Earth shrine, *tenga*, is usually found outside the walls of the patriclan residence of the priest. Like the shrine to the ancestral spirits, it is located on a barren spot of earth, but is rarely enclosed by any sort of structure. Occasionally the area is marked off by a ring of small stones. The altar itself is composed of a pile of small stones, upon which is placed a clay vessel, *tensaare*, approximately a foot in diameter and eight inches in depth. In this vessel are piled the *teense*, a term that means simply "things of the earth"—sticks and stones, bits of metal, pieces of broken pottery, and the remnants of lost and unclaimed property.

It is on this altar, with the Earth hoe and Earth staff laid across it, that sacrificial libations of flour and water, beer, or the blood of animals are poured as the priest calls the deity's attention to the offering and conveys whatever message is appropriate. Sacrifices are made both as part of the annual cycle of ceremonials that mark each phase of the year and at the request of particular supplicants who seek special supernatural assistance with their farm work or expiation for some transgression against the ritual sanctity of the Earth. Afterward the remainder of the libation, or the slain animal itself, is prepared by the priest's wives, to be consumed by him and his family.

The role of the Mossi Earth priest appears to be very much like that of the Earth "custodian" found among the Tallensi and Konkomba and related peoples living to the south of Yatenga, in the northern regions of the Ivory Coast, Ghana, and Togo. Among these people, all of whom lack centralized political systems, the exercise of the Earth priest's religious role is accompanied by the assertion of considerable authority. He has the right to intervene in disputes between residents of the ritual area, the right to punish a variety of crimes, and the capacity to restore social order through

ritual expiation and the levying of fines. The extent of the Earth
priest's authority and the frequency with which it is exerted appear
to be significantly related to the absence of alternative sources of
social control. It seems likely that prior to the establishment of a
centralized political system in Yatenga, the Earth priests there
were also possessed of considerably more political power than they
have today.[5]

While the Mossi Earth priests are charged with ritual propitiation
of the terrestrial and climatic manifestations of the deity, a separate
group, regarded as subordinate and auxiliary to them, has ritual
responsibility for maintaining balance in the Mossi's relation to
the third important natural manifestation of the deity, Tido Wende,
the vegetal aspect of the Mossi supreme being. Tido Wende is
worshipped through the intermediary role of the priests called
Bogaba.[6] Through them communication with the aspect of the deity
manifested in the vigor of plant growth is maintained. Ki Wende,
the Millet deity, is the still more specific natural aspect of the
supreme being with which the Bogaba are concerned. Theirs also
is the principal sacerdotal role in the observance of the Mossi
harvest ceremony, Tido, described in the next chapter. The Boga
can also assist barren women to conceive. A woman who makes
a sacrifice to Tido Wende and is granted a child names it after the
deity and should return each year with a sacrifice at harvest time in
order to continue the good relationship that brought an end to her
barrenness and to assure the continued good health of her child.

Many aspects of the status of the Bogaba parallel that of the
Earth priests. They are also sib elders. The shrine, *Tido Rogo*, to

5. *Ibid.*, p. 12.
6. *Boga* is the singular of this term. I was unable to find out exactly
what it means. My best guess is that it is derived from the Yatenga
mŏré version of the Ouagadougou *mŏré* word *boghe* which means "to
dissolve in water," "to be inundated," as from a heavy rain (G.
Alexandre, *La Langue Mŏré*, Dakar: Institut Français d'Afrique Noire,
1953, 2 vol., p. 52), and that it is thus suggestive of the natural event
for which these religious functionaries are responsible—lush and
abundant plant growth. Most Bogaba are smiths. And the smiths also
have the tradition of having inhabited the Yatenga prior to the Mossi
occupation. For this reason, and also because they are workers of
metal, they share with the descendants of the Nyonyose an especially
close relation to the Earth.

the vegetal manifestation of the deity is located outside the walls of their patriclan residence and also consists of a cleared area about six feet in diameter. The altar, *robogo*, itself, however, does not take the form of a clay vessel, but is simply a spot of raised earth over which libations are poured.

Like the Earth priests, the principal ritual accoutrements of the Bogaba are a staff and a hoe which are crossed upon the altar to receive the sacrificial libations. However their ceremonial dress is more elaborate than that of the Earth priests. They wear at all times a necklace of rolled leather studded with cowry shells and containing a single large stone bead. On ritual occasions they also wear suspended from the waist horsetails and strips of leather with bells attached, a cowry-covered leather coat, and a leather cap.

Although the Boga is always the elder of the founding lineage of his sib, succession to his religious role does not automatically follow his assumption of authority within the kin group, but occurs as the result of changes in his personality which are regarded as being of supernatural origin. These usually occur some time after he has succeeded his deceased elder brother as head of the lineage, and is said to be preceded by withdrawal from leadership in the sib. After a period of actual seclusion he re-emerges during the month of Yalem (October or November, depending on changes in the calendrical cycle) and assumes his new sacerdotal role.

Although the Bogaba may sometimes bear the name of the sib of the Earth priests, Savadogo, most belong to the indigenous lineages of metalworkers. If so, they usually have the sib names Zorom, Kindu, or Zebere. Like all smiths, they observe caste endogamy. The manner in which their status is subordinate to that of the Earth priests is best demonstrated in the performance of their ritual duties within the context of the Mossi ceremonial cycle described in the next chapter.

THE ANCESTORS

The *keemse,* the spirits of the ancestors of the Mossi, vitalize the second principal dimension of the supernatural milieu. The sense in which this supernatural environment is seen as one of the several equally orderly dimensions of reality—and as a projection of social experience—is well illustrated by the beliefs of the Mossi about their ancestors, and their ideas about what they ought to do to get along with their spirits. The Mossi believe that in the afterlife the spirits of the deceased members of the descent group maintain their interest in their living descendants, continue to look out for their well-being, and to be concerned with their behavior just as they were when they were the living elder members of the kin group. For this reason the spirits of those who have died at an advanced age are most important. The status of the spirits of deceased young adults is reflective of their subordinate position in life. The spirits of dead children are not important at all, because they will be born again sooner or later.

The rights and obligations that unite the living members of the sib and its component lineages are paralleled in their relationship to the spirits of their patrilineal and matrilineal kin: Patrilineal antecedents are more important, just as are their living agnates. When pressed to rationalize this patrilateral emphasis, the Mossi are no more successful than other people in explaining their own institutions. They usually say that it is because it is the man who takes the initiative in intercourse and "puts the seed" into the woman that the physical substance of the child is derived from him. The man's ancestors give the child its soul, *shiga*, and the spirits of the patrilineage watch over its growth and development throughout life. One of them, often father's father or a person of his generation, acts as the newborn infant's special protective spirit, and is called *masam soba*, which means literally "shade person," referring to the manner in which this protective spirit is believed to shield them from the harsher aspects of life, just as his elders protect him economically and socially.

Like all viable relationships among the Mossi, the tie to the ancestors is reciprocal. A child's father's father, as head of the extended household, bears some responsibility for his grandson's material well-being and, when necessary, intercedes for him with the ancestral spirits. When the child matures and his grandfather dies, it is his grandson who will remember him longest and see that sacrifices continue to be made to him.

Because the relation between a child and his father's father is more permissive than his relation to his own father or the members of his father's generation, it is believed that this permissiveness is perpetuated after father's father's death, when his spirit and the spirits of the men of his generation continue to watch with affectionate concern over the life activities of their grandchildren and those of their generation. When the Mossi refer casually to the ancestral spirits, they always call them *yaba namba,* "the grandfathers."

The role of the spirits of the agnatic descent group is protective in two senses: They look out for the well-being of their descendants, and they are equally concerned with the maintenance of tradition. They are the sources of good health and good fortune necessary for success at any pursuit, and they punish with sickness and occasionally death those who defy their prohibitions against incest, theft from a kinsman, bodily aggression toward a lineage mate, failure to respect the sib totem, and any other action damaging either directly to the kin group or indirectly to its status in the community.

The ancestral spirits can contribute to their descendants' well-being in many ways. They can send them good health, assist them in assuring the fertility of their fields and the abundance of the rains, and help their wives to conceive. In short they complement, supernaturally, the interests and action of the elder living kinsmen toward the social and economic activities of their younger relatives. Just as in life the lineage elders assist the more youthful members of the lineage with land, labor, assistance, advice and training, and a measure of political and religious protection. This generalized benevolence continues after death.

When the ancestors assist wives of lineage members to conceive, the children are given names that acknowledge their parents' gratitude. Such names as *Keem Bilo,* "Ancestor's Child," or *Keem Dawgo,* "Ancestor's Man," are examples. And just as the ancestral spirits can reward the wife of a member of the lineage by sending her a child, they can also punish her if she fails to meet her responsibilities as a wife. Thus when a woman miscarries or a child is stillborn or dies soon after birth, it is often believed the ancestral spirits are punishing her in this way for some transgression. Severe labor pains are also regarded as punishment by a woman's husband's ancestral spirits, a factor that explains the silence of Mossi women in labor. It is also felt that a woman in childbirth should not cry out so that the spirits will know she is grateful for the infant they have sent.

Those who anger the ancestral spirits and do not confess their transgressions and seek ritual expiation risk death. Even after confessing, persons guilty of particularly serious crimes, such as incest, still risk expulsion from the lineage. And the ancestral spirits then punish with sickness any member of the kin group who has further dealings with them. Smallpox is believed to be a disease particularly favored as a punishment by the ancestors. But their irritation can manifest itself in the development of any physical infirmity. Such punishment is not necessarily immediate. Sometimes it is necessary for the lineage elder to sacrifice a chicken to remind the ancestors of their responsibility.

It is only the spirits of those who have occupied positions of importance in the lineage—such as former lineage elders—who receive extensive sacrifices and take important action in the affairs of their descendants. Among these spirits, that of the founding ancestor of the sib is the most powerful. He commands such great respect that neither his name, if it is known, nor his proper kinship term, *sigiri,* can be used. In accordance with the patterned indirection always employed by the Mossi in dealing with socially important or emotionally or supernaturally charged phenomena, this first ancestor is referred to as *kikirigo,* which means twin. This is because although the Mossi twin spirits, the *kikirdisi,* are much less awe-inspiring than the ancestral spirits, they have analogous powers. They may send sickness or good fortune, and they also can steal the soul from a neighboring stand of millet to enrich the harvest of a farmer who has made sacrifices to them. The use of their name as a substitute for that of the more powerful apical ancestor of the descent group is deferential. It serves to attract his attention without the mention of his dangerously powerful name, an impropriety that might result in punishment. Such indirection is a manifestation of the recognized need for caution in dealing with a powerful being whose actions—once he is aroused—can be neither fully anticipated nor controlled.

On ritual occasions the ancestral spirits are propitiated on the basis of seniority—that is, in terms of their relative remoteness. While the spirit of the sib founder is the most powerful ancestral deity, the spirits of father's father's generation are regarded as having the closest relationship to mature members of the lineage and the greatest specific effect upon their lives and activities.

Control in relation to the ancestral spirits is achieved both through direct ceremonial propitiation and through adherence to the code of proper conduct that the ancestors established by their own example.

Sacrifices take place at special ancestral shrines. The shrine located in the residence of the headman of the founding lineage of the sib is called *rokyengo,* which means old and important house. The shrines located in the other lineage residences are called, in the singular, simply *keemse rogo,* or house of the spirits of the dead. According to tradition these shrines should be comprised of an inverted earthenware pot over which the sacrificial offerings are to be made. And this pot should be contained within a small house. In fact such houses are rarely encountered. Most often the ancestral shrine is a dome of hardened earth about two feet in diameter, slightly raised, and partially surrounded by a low circle of disintegrating mud bricks, the remnants of a house long since fallen into disrepair.

Any assumption that such apparent neglect were a manifestation of decreasing significance of ancestor worship among the Mossi should be tempered with recognition that most ritual areas and objects are treated by them with what appears to be an almost purposive casualness.

Although ancestral shrines are usually located near the center of the patriclan residence beside the house of the lineage elder, shifts from generation to generation in the precise arrangement of the dwellings comprising the residence sometimes result in leaving the shrine outside the walls at some distance from the kin group's present abode.

Chickens are most often used as sacrifices to the ancestors. Because goats and sheep are more costly, they are sacrificed only rarely. Millet beer and *zom kom,* a mixture of uncooked millet flour and water, are used for libations. Animals to be sacrificed are held over the shrine. As their throats are slowly cut, the ancestral spirits are greeted with words of thanks and praise, and attention is called to the fact that their descendants continue to follow traditional custom in making these offerings to them. Then the specific name of the donor of the animal is pronounced. If he has a request to make to his ancestors, this is stated. Otherwise the spirit or spirits addressed are simply thanked for their benevolence in the past,

". . . *keemse rogo* . . . house of the spirits of the dead."

and the sacrifices made to them are indicated as thanks also for
their protection in the future. After the blood has fallen on the
shrine, the dead animal itself is thrown aside to be cooked and
eaten later by all participants in the ceremony.

Sacrifices to the ancestral spirits can be made at any time.
Younger members of the kin group, however, must request the
permission of the lineage elder before offerings can be made on
their behalf. Sacrifices are made on the occasion of most transitions
in individual status. Often they are made prior to conception. They
are always made at birth and as a part of the ceremonies that mark
the attainment of puberty, marriage, and death. They can also be
made on the occasion of any important undertaking—before a
journey or some new economic task is begun or before seeking a
wife. And they are also made when a person falls ill. A man can
make a sacrifice for himself or in behalf of his wife or child. When
a specific request is made to the ancestral spirits, usually only a
chicken is sacrificed. If the request is important, the ancestors are
usually promised the sacrifice of a more valuable animal if their
request is granted. Then the supplicant returns later with a further
offering, usually a goat or a sheep.

Women participate more directly in the worship of the ancestral
spirits of their own descent groups. Older women, especially those
whose advanced years and many children have brought them more
important status, often return to their natal patriclans to make
sacrifices to their own ancestors and to assist their male kinsmen on
important ritual occasions. Elderly widows who frequently resume
permanent residence with their agnatic kinsmen—especially if they
have no male children—often assume direction, with their senior
agnates, in the preparation of food and beer for ceremonial
occasions involving the ancestors. Women can also ask that sacrifices be made for them to the spirits of their husbands' lineage.
Most often such sacrifices are made with the request that they be
sent a child, or to remind the ancestral spirits of an absent son,
thus preserving his relation to them until he returns.

The ancestral spirits of the Mossi dwell in *keem koulogou*, the
place of the dead, understood only to be in the general vicinity of
the lineage residence. They do not follow their descendants when
they leave their home communities and, outside Yatenga, they can
offer them no protection at all.

Sister's son's intermediary role in the performance of the sacrifices to the ancestors has already been described. His more permissive relationship with the spirits of his mother's patrilineage functions to assure that any defect in ceremonial protocol—the offering of a scraggly chicken or a too extravagant request—will be excused. He himself can make use of this relationship: A sacrifice or request he might hesitate to make to his own patrilineal ancestral spirits for fear of its impropriety can be made to the ancestral spirits of his mother's patrilineage with much greater likelihood of a favorable response.

Although children do not participate actively in the ceremonial propitiation of their ancestors, they are encouraged by their elders to observe all that occurs on ritual occasions, and details of the ceremonial are pointed out to them. They are not, however, on this or any other occasion formally instructed in the performance of ritual actions or in the rationale, the beliefs about the supernatural, that underlie such actions. If they directly question their elders, they are either told to be silent or are shamed by receiving an explanation intended to make them appear ridiculous. In this way they are instructed to respect tradition and to follow it without question. Adherence to tradition, not comprehension of it, is the way to supernaturally assured security.

For the Mossi the ancestral spirits are an intrinsic part, historically and contemporaneously, of the kinship system. Ancestors founded the system and established by their own comportment the pattern for correct conduct in all aspects of life. As the guardians of the social system and of their descendants' status within it, the ancestral spirits represent the final extension, into the supernatural, of the durable protective canopy of kinship relations which from birth to death and after provides for the Mossi's well-being.

ISLAM

Until recently the Mossi of Yatenga were remarkable among the peoples of the Western Sudan in their resistance, or, rather, their indifference, to Islam. Now its importance is growing rapidly. The negative response of the Mossi to Islam in the past relates most importantly to the nature of their traditional technology and its integration with the other aspects of their culture, and to the history of their relations with neighboring peoples.

The farming technology of the Mossi remained relatively unchanged even during the period of French occupation. Yatenga is a poor country in known mineral resources, in apparent agricultural potential, and in manufactures; it was and has remained "underdeveloped." As a consequence, traditional religious sanctions have retained their functional relevance to the traditional organization and performance of work, and to the accompanying organization of social and political relations. There has been no need for religious change.

With the gradual growth in importance of market exchange, however, the importance of Islam has increased. Because Moslem conversion provides a valuable justification for avoiding the most rigid aspects of authority based on the principle of Mossi kinship. A young man who identifies himself as a Moslem is expected to be more lax in terms both of economic and social cooperation with his kinsmen and in assisting economically with the regular sacrifices to the ancestral spirits. He is also excused from direct participation in the other ceremonials that mark the indigenous Mossi ceremonial calendar. However this break with the traditional religious system need not be, and rarely is, total.

Through the intermediary of a sister's son such a person's security within the indigenous supernatural order can be indirectly maintained. The same system of indirection that characterizes the reliance of the rest of the patrilineage on the intercession of sister's son in sacrifices to the ancestral spirits may be relied on by a Moslem convert. By making an occasional present to father's sister's son, the latter can be relied upon to intercede on his behalf with the ancestral spirits. Thus a young man can—if he needs to—escape from the responsibility of rigid adherence to the requirements of social and economic cooperation with his kinsmen by espousing Islam. At the same time he may be assured of the indirect perpetuation of his benevolent relationship to the traditional, kinship-based sources of his supernatural security.

With the inheritance of a position of property and status in the lineage that comes with advancing age, both Islam and the socioeconomic independence it justifies are often abandoned for resumption of full social and ceremonial participation in the kin group, and in the traditional kinship system.

The current success of Islam in Yatenga may also be related to the manner in which it allows for the achievement of status. Within the traditional religious system the assumption of religious roles is dependent upon kinship. Only men who are senior members of major lineages in sibs having the prerogative for assuming the role of Earth priest or Boga can hope to assume these important religious positions. In relationship to the ancestral spirits, the possibility of religious participation is equally minimal, for the assumption of the role of intermediary between the lineage and the ancestors is dependent upon seniority within the lineage. Sorcerers and diviners are the only participants in the traditional religious system who can assume a religious or magical role in the absence of any specific ascribed criteria.

In contrast, Islam offers an opportunity for the achievement of social prominence as well as changed religious status. It provides an opportunity to escape from the rigidly imposed authority of the lineage elders and, as a consequence, to enjoy as an individual the fruits of personal economic endeavor and social success. Those who establish themselves as Moslem holy men move away from their patriclan dwellings and establish separate households. There they often accept Koranic students who lodge with them and assist them economically by working in their fields and by begging. Later when these students go away as migrant laborers, they send back gifts to their Moslem sponsors. Thus by establishing himself as a holy man, a Mossi can escape from the limitations of junior status within a social system in which position is largely ascribed on the basis of seniority and kinship affiliation. He also acquires an ideological justification for ceasing to share his higher social status and greater wealth with his kinsmen. Through his students or followers he is provided with an advantageous alternative to his kin group. Most Mossi villages now have a small group of Moslems led by one or more *marabouts*. Very often these men are the ambitious junior members of their lineages, individuals whose social and economic ambitions could not be as readily realized by traditional means.

Conversion to Islam among the Mossi is facilitated by the minimal emphasis placed on the internationalization of Moslem theology. For a man to establish himself as a marabout, all that is necessary is a short period of apprenticeship with another marabout. He must be able to perform the motions of the five daily prayers, give instructions in their more or less proper pronunciation in Arabic, and use the Moslem prayer beads, know the feast days and times of fast, and assume a Moslem name. The observance of these outer forms of Islamic usage is all that is required. They can be learned either through residence with a local marabout or acquired in the more prestigeful context of a stay of several years in one of the cities of the Western Sudan—Bamako, Mopti, or Segou—where the impact of Islam has so far been more profound.

The fact that the Mossi are polytheistic and somewhat parochial is probably also important in explaining the ease with which conversion to Islam is achieved. They perceive the supernatural as vitalized by a variety of beings and forces. And they recognize the probable equal efficacy of the religious systems of their traditionally non-Moslem neighbors. Consequently the acceptance of Islam does not require total emotional and intellectual rejection of previously held religious ideas and practices. As with most West African peoples, this facilitates reinterpretation and syncretism, thus making an accelerated rate of religious change less disruptive.

For the convert to Islam without ambitions for leadership the process is still simpler. He need only assume a Moslem name, Mamadou, Salaam, and Boukari are especially popular—appear at the appropriate times with sand on his forehead and the tip of his nose as evidence that he has said his prayers, abstain from heavy drinking in public, and he will be accepted as a brother in Islam.

A further factor of significance for an understanding of the growth of Islam among the Mossi relates to the breakdown of barriers to intertribal and interterritorial travel that resulted from the establishment of the French colonial peace. Travel was stimulated by the imposition of a money tax which made it necessary for the Mossi to sell their labor and by the establishment of plantations along the coast and the development of commercial centers in the Western Sudan itself. Outside their homeland the profession of Islam served, and continues to serve, to unite people whose languages and tribal identities would otherwise set them apart. For the traditional intepretation of the role of foreigner among the Mossi

". . . the convert to Islam need only . . . appear at the
appropriate times with sand on his forehead and the tip
of his nose . . ."

bears no requirement for cooperation. A non-Mossi stranger traveling alone among them can anticipate either open hostility or indifference from those whose cultural identity is different from his own.

For Mossi migrant laborers, conditioned as they are to rely heavily on the emotional satisfactions derived from interaction with their fellows, to be outside Yatenga is to find themselves isolated in the midst of a variety of social and supernatural forces that can be neither understood nor controlled. Under such circumstances the profession of Islam provides an alternative source of both social and supernatural security.

Thus there is a sense in which the traditional religion of the Mossi, based on the worship of nature and the ancestors, appears to be threatened. In isolation it could presumably continue to function well, but the result of contact beyond their own frontiers is leading the Mossi to economic opportunities which weaken the authority of the elders by providing young people with alternative sources of economic satisfaction based on a more individually orientated pattern of economic endeavor.[7] Islamization provides a rationalization for defection from the traditional kinship structure and its system of rights and obligations. In addition it can provide, as in the case of the Mossi marabout, not only freedom from traditional economic responsibilities, but also a lucrative alternative source of economic and social status.

The relation between religious beliefs and practices of the Mossi and the other aspects of their culture is clear. Essentially their religion has derived its reason for being and its basic forms and functions from the nature of the natural environment of Yatenga and from the adjustment—technological, economic, social, and political—the Mossi have achieved to this environment. Certain specifics of these basic forms and functions are, of course, to be explained historically.

This contention will be further validated if religious change in Yatenga continues to follow, as it has so far, from the technological innovations and economic changes that appear to be an inevitable aspect of the destiny of all "underdeveloped" areas. Yatenga included.

7. For more on the ideological consequences of technological and economic change among the Mossi see Hammond (1959, 1963).

CHAPTER EIGHT

THE CYCLE OF THE MOSSI YEAR

The manner in which the Mossi of Yatenga perceive their relation to the forces, both social and supernatural, that vitalize their milieu is most explicitly reified in the yearly technological cycle and the rituals that accompany each of its phases. This ceremonial cycle is strikingly reflective of the integration of virtually all aspects of Mossi culture and of the important role of technology in determining the essential patterning of this integration. It illustrates also the consequent coherence of their view of the world and of the actions they must take in order to maintain their well-being within it.

The inception of each of the several phases of the Mossi technological cycle is dependent upon the climatic conditions that affect the growth of their crops. The ceremonies that mark each of these phases must be adjusted accordingly. As a result the beginning of the ceremonial cycle and its duration vary from year to year. Usually the Mossi calendar is divided into twelve moons, the names of which refer either to the principal technological activity that then occurs or to the accompanying ritual observance. A description of this cycle can only be approximate, for the people of each village vary the calendar somewhat to adjust to local variation in growing conditions. As a result the same technological activities and their accompanying rituals may occur in different lunar months in different parts of the country.

The first moon of the Mossi year is called *Gambo* after the village which celebrates the rain-making ceremonial, *Tengana*, soon after it appears. Although the rains are still five or six months away, Tengana marks the beginning of the new growing cycle and is the first ritual step taken to reaffirm man's relation to the supernatural forces that order those aspects of his natural environment upon which he is dependent for his success as a farmer. Tengana may be celebrated either in January during the Gambo moon, in February, as it is at the old village of Zonduma which gives its name to the second moon of the new year, or, as in the village of Gourcy, it can be observed in the third moon, called *Gourcy Tengana.*

At Gourcy, Tengana is celebrated on the seventh day of the new moon. In preparation men give their wives small-grained millet to grind into flour which is mixed with water to make *zom kom,* the cereal gruel used in sacrificial libations. On the morning of the ceremony each patriclan sends a young girl with an offering of millet gruel to the Earth priest in charge of the ritual area within which their farmlands are located. These offerings, contained in small clay bowls, are placed by the Earth shrine. At midmorning, when all the offerings have arrived, the Earth priest takes up each small container and pours its contents over the altar, calling out to the Earth deity, Tenga Wende, the name of the kin group from which the offering comes and—as is always the custom when the Mossi make sacrifices—explicitly stating that the offering is given in thanks for the success of the past year's harvest and in thanks in advance for the heavy rains and good growing conditions of the season to come. As each offering is poured out, all the other small girls sent by their kinsmen hold out their clay bowls to catch some of the libations as they fall, to mix with their own, thereby "capturing" a part of the goodness of the harvests of others.

When all the offerings have been received, the Earth priest takes up a small part of the wet earth on which the sacrificial libations have been poured and places it in each girl's bowl. This soil represents the now-sanctified soul of the millet. The small clay vessels

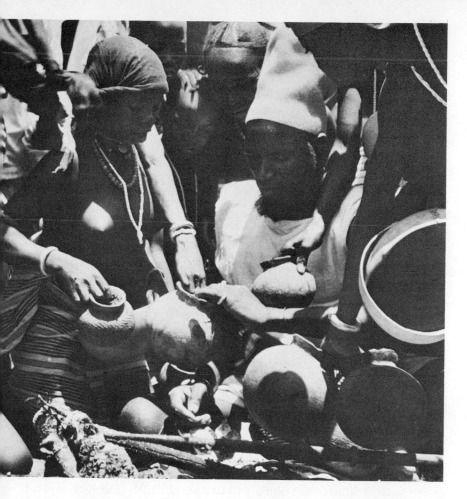

". . . the other small girls . . . hold out their clay bowls to catch some of the libations as they fall . . ."

containing it are then returned to each patriclan residence to be placed under a granary belonging to the lineage elder, the one from which millet seeds for his new crop will be taken.

Later the same day men from all the lineages with farmland under the ritual control of the Earth priest organize a hunt. When they return in the early evening, their catch is offered to him. He takes a portion for himself and the members of his household and returns the rest to the hunters. No part of this game is sacrificed; the hunt is a tributary service, to recompense the Earth priest for ceremonial services rendered and as an advance assurance of the continued support of those who work land under his ritual control.

The day following the observance of Tengana the Earth priest visits each of the patriclan residences within his ritual area. On arrival he first seats himself either at the door or in the courtyard of the dwelling of the lineage elder, whose first wife greets him, followed by the other older members of the patriclan. Then the senior wives bring calabashes filled with millet gruel. The lineage elder places these in the hands of the Earth priest who pours out their contents over the crossed hoe and staff, the symbols of his ritual status. He asks the Earth deity to grant good health, heavy rains, and a successful harvest to the patriclan elder and to the other members of his kin group. At this time individual farmers in the family often speak up requesting the assistance of Tenga Wende with a particular crop, such as cotton or beans. And often they add offerings of millet beer to these libations of millet gruel. Here, also, as the offerings are poured out each woman in the patriclan tries to catch a little of the liquid in her own calabash, and then pours it out herself in order to capture for her own fields some of the good fortune that has been enjoyed by others in the patriclan. In this way the Earth priest moves about all day, visiting successively all the lineages that possess land under his control. At evening the several Earth priests of the community gather at the residence of the village chief to make the same sacrifice a final time. Then the wives of the village chief offer the Earth priests a meal, thus demonstrating once more the reciprocal tie between the sources of political and supernatural power. With this Tengana is concluded.

The observance of the Tengana ritual is believed to have both a specific and a general function—specifically to assure the fertility of the soil and also to perpetuate the generalized benevolence of the earthly manifestation of the deity. For as in all Mossi rituals, the emphasis is not alone on the specific supernatural function of the deity but upon man's reliance on all the more diffuse aspects of his supernatural power as well. Particular supplications regarding the rains or soil fertility are always accompanied by general requests for social order, good health, and good fortune for all the kin group. This in recognition of the fact that the deity in his several inter-related manifestations possesses the power to effect men's lives in many ways, both direct and indirect, known and unknown.

The moon that follows Gourcy Tengana is called *Bega* after the ceremonial that marks the second phase in the Mossi technological cycle and the first work in the fields—the cleaning, clearing, and burning of dried brush and other rubbish that precedes planting. The ritual purpose of Bega is the propitiation of the vegetal manifestation of the deity, Tido Wende. Usually this activity coincides with the European calendar month of April. At the Bega ceremony the Earth priest first makes a sacrifice at the Earth shrine and then goes to the residence of the Boga, the priest charged with the auxiliary role of intercession with the aspect of the deity responsible for plant growth. This visit symbolizes the interdepend-ent relationship of the two ritual roles and the complementary quality of the particular sources of supernatural powers with which they are respectively concerned.

Following the visit of the Earth priest the Boga sets out from his household to follow the course taken by the Earth priest at Tengana the month before, visiting successively the compound residence of each patriclan which works land within the Earth priest's ritual domain. The sacrifice follows the same sequence. But on this occasion the offerings are made not to the Earth but to Tido Wende, the supernatural force that gives life to all things growing on the land. For seven nights following the Bega sacrifices the young unmarried girls of each patriclan in the village gather outside their compound residences to clap their hands and dance, clearly expressing in their songs the mood and expectations of the season.

> This year is sweet,
> Next year will be sweeter still.

> The household head will be there where the earth is
>   moist.

His children will be abundant, as the cotton bush is
    covered with flowers,
There will be no end to harvesting them.

The rains will fall,
The water will rush through the valleys,
The parched earth will be drenched, the low lands
    white with water.

Children will run joyously in the rain.

Or

I need someone to shake the heavy branches of my
    shea nut tree.

I have already seen the branches are full of fruit,
But I cannot gather them alone . . .

Following the Bega sacrifices the Mossi farmers go out to their
fields and prepare them for the planting which will begin after the
first heavy rain.

When the fields have been cleared and are ready to be seeded, a
sacrifice is made to Pogo Wende, a particular aspect of the Earth
deity present in each man's fields. This is an individual observance
and may precede or follow the sowing of the first seeds. Several
days before the sacrifice is to be made, the farmer visits the Earth
priest to ask for ritual assistance. On the day agreed upon the Earth
priest goes into the farmer's fields accompanied by the members of
the farmer's household. There he is presented with a sheep or a goat
which he sacrifices to Pogo Wende, making the usual request for
good health, heavy rains, and a rich harvest. The blood of the slain
animal is allowed to run out over the earth. Then a portion of the
animal itself is prepared and cooked by the women and eaten in the
field. The hide and a part of the carcass that remains are then
offered to the Earth priest as payment for his services.

This sacrifice is designed to enlist not only the benevolence of
the specific manifestation of the deity present on the farmer's land
but also the twin spirits, *kikirdisi*, which often dwell in a man's
fields. If these spirits are well disposed toward the farmer, they
will protect the soul of his millet crop from the twin spirits of a
neighboring field who might otherwise try to steal it to increase

"For seven nights following the Bega sacrifices, the young unmarried girls . . . gather outside the compound residence to clap their hands and dance . . ."

the yield of their own patron's crop. Like the spirits of the ancestors, the twins steal the souls of a stand of grain by sending a high wind. When the unripe seeds are blown from the millet heads, their souls are released and can be captured.

The moon following Bega is called *Cundiba Bega*, after the village that observes the Bega ceremonial when it first appears. Usually the Cundiba Bega moon is first seen in the month of May. By this time most of the Mossi farmer's fields are fully planted. The moon that next appears is called *Kizale*, which means "unaccompanied," in reference to the fact that its appearance, literally, is unaccompanied by any calendrical rituals. During this period the Mossi villages are nearly deserted throughout the day, with all the able-bodied members of every household away in the fields.

The next moon is called *Budibo*, a term that means first seeding and refers to the crops sown after the millet is in—the beans, groundnuts, and melons often interplanted with millet and also the cotton, tobacco, and other crops planted later in the growing season. The moon following Budibo is called *Waraga*, in reference to the first cultivation of the millet fields which, by this time, is usually well underway.

The following moon appears in late August or early September and is called *Baka*, after the term used to designate the second cultivation. If the millet is not yet ripe for harvest at the appearance of the moon which follows, it also is called *Baka*. Some Mossi farmers cultivate a third time during this period.

The decision to call this new moon *Baka* and continue with cultivation, or to call it *Yalem* and begin the harvest rests with the chief of Rom, a village which served as a temporary residence of the founding king of Yatenga, Naba Yadega. Just behind the residence of the village chief at Rom is a sacred millet field. The "souls" of the millet grains from this field are believed to have a special supernatural relation to the spirits of the past kings of Yatenga, the *reem sheese*. If the millet in this field is ripe when the new moon following Baka appears, the lunar period is called *Yalem* and marks the beginning of the final phase of the ceremonials that close the technological cycle of the Mossi year. All of Yatenga must wait on the decision of the chief at Rom in order to know whether the round of ceremonials, called *Basga*, is to begin, or whether the harvest and its attendant rituals and festivities are to be put off for the duration of another moon.

In the early days of the Yatenga dynasty, millet from this field at Rom was used to prepare sacrificial libations for the spirits of the ancestors of the Yatenga Naba, the deceased former rulers of the newly established kingdom, the capital of which was then located in the nearby village of Gourcy. Now when they are cut the first millet heads from this sacred field are divided into three parts. One portion is used to prepare millet gruel to be offered to the spirits of the deceased kings at a shrine dedicated to them at Rom itself. This altar is located just outside the walls of the residence of the village chief. The remaining two portions of millet are then put into separate leather bags. One is sent to the Yatenga Naba at Ouahigouya, the present capital. The other is sent to Gourcy, the ancient capital. The emissaries are accompanied as they walk off toward Ouahigouya and Gourcy by young people who break off stalks of millet from the fields along the way and add them to the bundles of grain from the sacred field at Rom. In this way all the farmers of Yatenga participate symbolically in these offerings which reify the dependence of the Mossi on the continued benevolence of the souls of the dead kings and serve to assure the farmers' continued well-being. The millet taken to Ouahigouya is sacrificed at the palace shrine to the spirits of the former rulers. At Gourcy the millet is used in the preparation of a sacrificial libation made at the ancestral shrine located on the site of the early kings' residence. A small portion of the millet received at Gourcy is also used to make a sacrifice to the ancestors of the present Gourcy chief.

At Ouahigouya and Gourcy a part of each sacrificial offering of millet is further divided, and portions are sent to other villages important in the political history of the Yatenga—to Lago, Kassuka, and Oula. A final portion, along with a tributary gift of salt from the Yatenga Naba and the chief at Gourcy, are returned to Rom with millet stalks from the local crop at each place. These are used to make a last sacrifice at Rom, one which symbolizes the inter-dependent relation between the Mossi villages and the powerful spirits of their former chiefs, and also manifests indirectly the integration between the technological, political, and religious aspects of the Mossi cultural milieu.

The role of the spirits of these dead Mossi kings is analogous to the role of the ancestral spirits of the kin group. They watch over their living descendant, the Yatenga Naba, and his subjects and provide the good health and social peace necessary for the conduct of the many tasks related to the subsistence technology. So long as these spirits protect the king, guard his health, and support him in his political role, the well-being of his people is assured.

At the conclusion of the Basga rituals Mossi farmers go into their fields and begin the harvest.

The ceremony that follows Basga is called *Kom Filiga*, Water Thanksgiving, and serves to symbolize and perpetuate the reliance of the Mossi on the Yatenga Naba himself. Kom Filiga, which usually occurs later in October or in early November, is the occasion for thanking the king for his wise direction of affairs which has permitted them to cultivate their fields in peace. In the preceding ritual, Basga, the king's ancestors were thanked for their supernatural support. Kom Filiga parallels this, and the living chief receives tribute also, in recognition of his power, as a recompense for his political services, and as a means of assuring their perpetuation. For this ceremony the chiefs of important villages in Yatenga travel to Ouahigouya to pay the Yatenga Naba tribute and to reassert their political allegiance to him—an allegiance in which the acceptance of the king's authority, especially by the important canton and village chiefs of Yatenga, is carefully accompanied by the symbolic assertion of their own semiautonomy.

Arriving in the capital the evening before, each Mossi chief, accompanied by a small retinue of village counselors, goes to the residence of the chief of his province, who is also always one of the Yatenga Naba's ministers. There he is received hospitably, makes gifts to his host, is served a fine meal, and settles down for the night. On the following afternoon the Yatenga Naba, accompanied by his ministers, the provincial chiefs, receives the village and canton chiefs outside the entrance to his palace. At the beginning of this ritual reception each of the chiefs, mounted on horseback, elegantly attired in a voluminous white cloak, and surrounded by his retainers, stands off from the king at a distance of several hundred yards. Servitors of the Yatenga Naba first approach the most important of the canton chiefs, Gourcy Naba. They kneel before him and present him with a welcoming calabash of millet gruel. This action represents the king's recognition of his need of the material and political support of the important local leaders and of their ancestors and communities.

In accepting this offering, Gourcy Naba first approaches the king on horseback accompanied by a small band of armed men, his counselors, and a drummer beating out proverbs alluding to the nobility of his descent. Riding down fiercely he reins in his mount just before the king and salutes him and the members of his household with a formal show of arrogance. Invoking the deity and the spirits of his ancestors, Gourcy Naba states firmly that in greeting the Yatenga Naba he is following in the traditional path, the one first established by his predecessors. His greeting is acknowledged by the king and Gourcy Naba rides off, dismounts, and pours out the millet gruel offered to him in a sacrifice to all the dead chiefs who have preceded him.

The Yatenga Naba is then approached in this same way, in symbolic half-defiance, by the chiefs of the important cantons of Lago, Kassuka, and Oula, whose ancestors assisted the first king, Naba Yadega, in founding Yatenga.

Following this first arrogant salutation, these same chiefs approach the king once more, this time on foot, moving slowly, bent forward, and pouring dust over their now uncovered heads as a mark of their submission. Each greets the Yatenga Naba again, and this time with a formal showing of great respect announces that he has brought him a sheep as tribute. The Yatenga Naba greets them in return, calling them by name, sending salutations to the people of their villages, and expressing his pleasure that they are continuing to follow the customs established by their ancestors. The sheep are then divided among the king's principal ministers and their followers, and the ceremony is concluded.

The Mossi refer to this ceremony, Kom Filiga, as the beginning of the king's new year. In recognition of the importance of this ceremonial in reaffirming the interdependence of the Yatenga Naba and his subjects, the years of his reign are counted from one Kom Filiga to the next.

Yalem, the lunar period in which Basga and Kom Filiga are observed, is followed by the moon called *Tido*. Its appearance marks the beginning of the ceremony designed to thank the deity, in his vegetal manifestations, for support during the growing season and for the harvests that have just been put away. The conduct of the

Tido rituals is directed by the Earth priests, but it is their auxiliaries, the Bogaba, who officiate. Throughout the duration of the Tido moon the Bogaba gather each evening in a different village to dance before the dwelling of the local Boga and assist him with the sacrifices to be made to the spirits of his deceased antecedents and to Tido Wende. On each occasion the first sacrifices are made to the ancestors of the living Boga, who offers several chickens to his deceased predecessors, those whose past ritual actions serve him as a guide and whose special supernatural powers augment his own. As the chickens' throats are slowly cut and their blood runs out over the altar of the shrine, these spirits are thanked for their support during the preceding year and their guidance is asked in the proper performance of the rituals of propitiation to Tido Wende which are soon to follow. Later the same evening the chickens offered to the ancestors are collected and cooked by the women of the host Boga's patriclan.

On the evening before, as the Boga and the elders of his kin group are engaged in making sacrifices to the spirits of the deceased Bogaba of their lineage, gifts are sent by the elders of patriclans that work land under the ritual control of the Earth priest to whom the Boga is auxiliary. These gifts of food, cloth, or tools are made in accordance with the carefully calculated emphasis on reciprocity characteristic of all Mossi transactions, and are intended as a material recompense to the Boga for the sacerdotal services he has rendered.

The sacrifices to Tido Wende take place the following morning. They are preceded by an initial offering of millet gruel made by the local Earth priest and by a brief visit made by the village chief who presents an animal for sacrifice, usually a sheep. Gathered outside the entrance to the residence of the Boga at the shrine to Tido Wende, the guest Bogaba are first thanked for their assistance with the ritual that is to follow. They then receive offertory libations for their ancestors in recognition of their support and of the continued importance after death of their particular supernatural prerogatives. As this offering is being poured before each Boga, he closes his eyes and begins to tremble: He is in the presence of his ancestors come to receive the sacrifice. As the tremors begin, a woman of the lineage of the host Boga steps quickly up to each one and loosens the cowry shell necklace, the *Bogalagafo*, which is his badge of

"Now at Filiga it is the ancestral members of each descent group . . . who are thanked . . ."

office transmitted to him by his deceased predecessor. This releases him from the vision of his ancestors. Following this the host Boga pours the remainder of the millet gruel over the altar, thanks Tido Wende for his benevolent cooperation throughout the past growing season, and asks for his continued protection in the year to come.

The wives of the members of the Boga's lineage, and all other women in the village who have conceived as a result of their prayers to Tido Wende, then go forward to offer the deity millet gruel in thanksgiving and in assurance of their continued dependence. Adults who believe themselves to have been conceived in response to their mothers' supplication to Tido Wende also make offerings of millet gruel. The host Boga then counsels all participants to be cautious and properly reverent in their use of the land and in their actions toward all things that grow upon it.

After a day's rest the several Bogaba go on to the village of another among them and there the Tido ritual is repeated. By this means at the conclusion of the growing season all communities in Yatenga ritually reaffirm their dependent relation to the Earth and to the plants that grow upon it and provide them a living.

The next ceremony in the Mossi ritual calendar is called simply *Filiga,* thanksgiving, and is celebrated at the appearance of the moon that follows Tido, usually in December. At Basga and Kom Filiga the king and his ancestral spirits were thanked for their contribution to the abundance of the harvests. Now at Filiga it is the ancestral members of each descent group, each sib and its component lineages, who are thanked for the protection they have provided for their descendants during the hard months of the past growing season. The sacrifices at Filiga are begun by the village chief, who makes offerings both at the separate altar dedicated to the spirits of the former chiefs and, if he is the elder of his lineage, also at the ancestral shrine located in the compound residence of his own patriclan.

The purpose of the sacrifice to the spirits of the dead chiefs at the outset of the Filiga ritual is not only to thank them for their benevolence during the preceding year, but also to enlist their assistance during the period of danger that is to follow. For at Filiga, when the ancestral spirits of the villagers will all receive the thanksgiving offerings of their descendants, they are believed to be much closer to the living members of their lineages and more likely to cause trouble for them if they are in any way dissatisfied with the ritual treatment they receive. They may try to call some of their descendants to join them or cause difficulty in a variety of other unpredictable ways, like the somewhat irascible old souls they are.

Filiga and the ceremony called *Na Poosum* which follows are occasions for social celebration as well. The crops are in, the granaries filled, and food is once more abundant after the frequent shortages that occur during the last weeks before the harvests. It is a time of leisure and pleasure. There is time for drinking and for boastful display at the gatherings that accompany the rituals of thanksgiving. Because such social occasions often lead to verbal disputes and physical aggression, the spirits of the former chiefs are evoked in the hope they will help to maintain order.

After this initial sacrifice to the spirits of the former chiefs the members of each descent group in the village gather to make sacrificial offerings to their own ancestral spirits. When several of the component lineages of the sib are located in the same village, the elders of each group first gather at the ancestral shrine of the founding lineage, after which each separate patriclan residence is visited in terms of its relative position in the chronology of lineage segmentation and fission.

As has been indicated, there is usually present in each Mossi patriclan residence the household of a sister's son, a member of mother's patrilineage. And it is usually this uterine kinsman who is called upon to intercede for his mother's agnates with the spirits of their ancestors. As the members of the lineage and their wives are seated around the ancestral altar, the sib elder presents the first chicken to a sister's son who cuts its throat slowly and offers it to the *kikirigo*, the twin, as the founding ancestor of the lineage is indirectly referred to.[1] A second chicken is presented to *sigiri*, the soul giver. This term is ordinarily used in reference to the spirit of a person of the generation of father's father's father. As it is used

1. In this way the mention of the name of a powerful supernatural being is avoided by reference to an entity with analogous but lesser powers. Like the ancestors, the twin spirits can also "send" children to Mossi women. Indirection as an avoidance mechanism is a characteristic attribute of Mossi patterns of communication and social interaction. I have also described this elsewhere. See Hammond 1959, 1963, and 1964.

here, it refers to all the ancestral spirits of his generation. The lineage elder then presents a chicken to be sacrificed to the grandfathers, the *yaba namba,* those belonging to the generation whose members died within memory of the living. Finally a chicken is offered by the headman to the *ba namba,* the fathers, the ancestral spirits of the deceased members of his own generation.

As each chicken's throat is slowly cut, the ancestors are thanked for their protection throughout the rainy season and requested to continue to look out for the welfare of their descendants during the months of the dry season to come. After the lineage elder has completed his offerings, his younger brothers follow, each in turn making his sacrifice to the ancestral spirits. Finally the younger men of the kin group approach to offer their sacrificial chickens. Usually they make offerings only to the spirits of the generation of father's father and to the ancestors of their father's generation. Chickens are also sacrificed in the name of absent kinsmen. Women in the patriclan often come forward as the ritual progresses and ask that a chicken be offered to the ancestors in the name of an absent son. This does not mean the Mossi have much confidence in the ability of the ancestors to protect those absent from Yatenga, but rather, that such a sacrifice helps to assure that the ancestral spirits will look out for their interests, especially their rights to land and the inheritance of property, while they are away, and that they will "remember them" when they return. Occasionally a chicken is also offered to the ancestors at the request of a member of the kin group who has become a Moslem but is not totally convinced of the equal efficacy of the new sources of supernatural control to which he has at least tentatively committed himself.

When the sacrifices are ended, the chickens themselves are prepared by the women and consumed at a communal feast the following day. Later in the afternoon there is much visiting, especially between in-laws, agemates and bond-friends. Ashes from the kitchen fires are spread at the entrances to the homes of the patriclan elders to invoke the continued benevolence of the ancestral spirits. Before entering one another's houses visitors call out, "May what you have received this year be granted to you in the season to come." Then they are invited in and served millet beer.

The final aspect of the ceremonial closing of the technological cycle is the observance called *Na Poosum,* chief's salutation. In

"The final aspect of the ceremonial closing of the technological cycle is the observance called *Na Poosum*, chief's salutation."

function it parallels Kom Filiga, the ritual occasion on which the Yatenga Naba is thanked for his role in maintaining societal order. Here the same ceremonial is observed in each village, canton, and province. At a village Na Poosum the elders of all the kin groups whose members comprise the local population pay tribute to the chief, making him gifts of millet and assuring him of their continued reliance upon his political power and intercession with his powerful ancestors in order that the village may enjoy peace throughout the coming months of the dry season and early rains at the beginning of the next year. Like the king at Kom Filiga, the chiefs at Na Poosum receive the representatives of the lineages of the community before the entrance to their residence and similarly greet the elders by name and commend their adherence to the ancestor's way.

At Gourcy, where the principal shrine to the first kings of Yatenga is located, the village chief takes a portion of the millet he has received to the elder of the kin group charged with maintaining the dead king's residence. There he enters the shrine to salute the spirits of the kings and to present his offering of grain. Like the millet he has received himself from the lineage elders of his own village and from the village chiefs of the canton under his command, this is regarded not as a sacrifice, but as a contribution to the maintenance of the former kings' shrine. The grain received is placed in the storehouses attached and used later in sacrificial libations. A portion is kept also by those who maintain the shrine.

With Na Poosum all of the sources of power—social, political, and supernatural—upon which the Mossi's well-being is dependent have been rewarded for their support throughout the past year and encouraged by the generosity of their supplicants to continue their benevolence through the season to come. The technological cycle has been completed; and the economic and social activities and the rituals that accompany it have also come to an end.

Many of the young men, who have no role of importance to play in these final rituals, leave soon after the harvests to seek work in Ghana, the Ivory Coast, or in the cities of the Western Sudan. The rest of the Mossi now turn their attention to necessary household repairs, to carpentry, and to brick making. Balls of cotton are brought out from their storage jars to be spun into thread and later woven into long strips of cloth. Craftsmen take up their specialities. The pottery kilns of the smiths are soon alight. Tools are made or mended. Marriages are arranged. And families in which a death has occurred during the growing season begin preparations for the funeral rituals which necessarily follow several months after their kinsman's quick interment. Visits are made to relatives and friends in other villages. Young mothers take their new babies home to see their families. And as the dry season progresses, long hours are spent in leisurely conversation under the sun shelters near the newly filled granaries.

CHAPTER NINE

TECHNOLOGY AS AN ASPECT OF MOSSI CULTURE

An understanding of the technology of the Mossi, or more explicitly, of the integration between the natural environment of Yatenga and the technological adjustment the Mossi have achieved to it, is essential for an adequate comprehension of the contemporary organization of their way of life and of their culture history. Such an understanding is equally essential to successful prediction of the ways in which Mossi culture is likely to change in the future.

Here attention has been focused on developing the central aspect of this contention—that an understanding of the nature of Mossi technology is critical to accurate assessment of the present structure and function of the other core aspects of Mossi culture: economic organization, social organization, political organization, and religion.[1]

1. In this book I have developed the idea within the context of the

TECHNOLOGY AND ECONOMIC ORGANIZATION

The primacy attached to redistribution and reciprocity as mechanisms for the allocation of both productive and consumption goods within Mossi economic organization is causally related to technological factors in several ways. First consider the question of land. Given the fragility of the relation between Mossi farming techniques and the poor soils and uncertain climate of the region, redistribution, complemented by reciprocity, provides a flexibility essential to the maintenance of balance in the relations between land, men, and the goods men produce on the land. The validity of this argument can be tentatively assessed by consideration of the probable effect of an alternative system. If, for example, land were owned privately and allocated through the market—the only currently feasible alternative to the present system of tenure in which land belongs first to the ancestors and the living members of the lineage and sib, with residual rights held by the chiefs and the Earth priests—those farmers whose particular fields had become dessicated and eroded or unusable for other reasons would risk becoming landless. And thereby unable to produce the goods essential to their material survival. Unable to produce any salable goods, they would have no means of acquiring money to purchase new land through the market. At the same time individuals and family groups which for any one of many possible reasons had become reduced in number would, in some instances, continue to hold lands in excess of their need. Such a process of land loss and accumulation would result in an increase of dysfunctional inequities in the distribution of productive goods that would quickly reduce a large part of the population to a subsubsistence level—a condition that would threaten the society's survival.

Thus, given the level and type of technological development among the Mossi, the only alternative to the present system for the allocation of productive goods would be one that, if it worked at all, would clearly work to the serious disadvantage of the Mossi majority. By such an analysis the teleology implicit in a purely structuralist exposition of interinstitutional integration is at least

traditional culture of the Mossi. However, the same processes were also operative among the Mossi settled at the Niger Project in Mali. See Hammond, 1959, 1960, and 1963.

partially replaced with a contention as to causality that can ultimately be tested. In short, it is argued that the economic system of the Mossi is organized as it is not only because such organization is eufunctional in its relation to the technology, but because it works better than any alternative system to meet the Mossis' cultural needs and thus to foster their survival. This is the principal reason for the development and persistence of the Mossi economic system so far.

The interrelationship between technology and that aspect of the Mossi economic system that relates to the organization of work is equally close. Again, the fragility of the technological adjustment and relatively low productivity appear to be the critical factors. If cooperative work based on the principles of redistribution and reciprocity is not absolutely essential at every phase of the productive cycle, it is, nonetheless, more efficient than any alternative kind of work organization.

Mossi women, for example, do much of the work of farming, yet there are times when they must have assistance because the work is too heavy, because they are pregnant, or because of their other household responsibilities. Again, alternatives to the prevailing system must be considered if the significance of its organization is to be assessed properly. If work were not so organized that there were a variety of others upon whom women could call for assistance—children, co-wives, husbands, and husbands' younger agnates—their harvests would frequently be less abundant and their crops would more often fail. The money income of Mossi women is usually not sufficient to permit them to hire laborers because most of the goods they produce are consumed by the members of their households and thus cannot be sold. Occasionally they can make enough from the sale of their surpluses to hire workers, but usually they cannot. When they could not, under a market system for the allocation of labor, their productivity would be decreased accordingly.

Mossi men are equally reliant on the cooperative assistance of others. Sickness, the desertion of their younger siblings or sons, or their involvement in other affairs in the community make it critical for them to have persons upon whom they can rely for help with the work on their farms. The same principle holds as for women farmers: The traditional technology, accompanied as it is by redistributive and reciprocal systems for the allocation of consumption goods, is not sufficiently productive to permit a farmer to employ wage laborers as often as he needs help. Reliance on the market for labor would, in this instance also, result in a potentially deleterious decrease in productivity.

In addition to the need for help to accomplish tasks on time, the Mossi contend that it is more agreeable, and thus more efficient, to work collectively and cooperatively with kinsmen and friends. While this factor is, perhaps, less compelling than the others, it is, nonetheless, generally evident that the prevailing system for the organization of work among the Mossi is to be explained not just by the fact that it "functions," but because, in relation to Mossi technology, it functions best.

That aspect of Mossi economic organization that provides for the distribution of consumption goods bears an equally close and causal relationship to the technology. Redistribution and the complementary role of reciprocity assure the equitable distribution of whatever food is available. Succinctly, no one is hungry unless most people—if not all people—are hungry. Under the market the only alternative system practicably possible, this would probably not be so. The individual farmer whose crops were to fail, or who fell sick during the growing season or at harvest time, would then be without food. He could survive only if he had in the past produced a surplus sufficient to feed his family for an additional year or large enough to be converted into cash adequate to purchase the food he needed. But Mossi technology is not sufficiently productive for this. Under the present system, by apparently subordinating his own personal economic interests to the interests of the group and thus assuring the cooperation of his kinsmen in time of need the Mossi farmer actually "maximizes" his chances for economic security. At the present level of Mossi technological development no other system could work as well to provide for the material security of the majority.

The potentially dysfunctional consequences of allocating consumption goods through the market is already apparent among the Mossi. If a man runs short of food before the harvest and cannot, for some still unusual reason, turn to his kinsmen for support, he is forced to borrow money to purchase grain. When money is most expensive he must borrow against the value of his future crop, and purchase grain at inflated preharvest prices. Then to avoid paying usurious interest he must meet his debt by selling a portion of his crop immediately after the harvest, when prices are lowest. Consequently he must sell a lot. Then he will probably not have enough food to last through the next year and he will probably have to borrow again. Probably more.

As a result of the efforts of the French colonial administration to stimulate participation in the market, with no regard for the delicate relationship between the economic system and the technology, this sort of imbalance has already begun to occur. If it continues without an accompanying increase in the productivity of the technology the present equitable distribution of material goods necessary for the satisfaction of the Mossis' basic needs will be seriously disrupted, with consequences which are easy, but unpleasant, to foresee.

Basically the market cannot serve satisfactorily as the principal locus and process for the allocation of either productive goods, labor, or consumption goods because Mossi technology is not sufficiently productive to provide the material surpluses that market exchange requires if it is to assure the satisfaction of the material needs of all members of the society. Perhaps for this reason the Mossi market has remained external to the operation of those institutional controls, based on kinship, association, religion, and the political system, that structure the organization of all activities within the context of the traditional culture. This absence of traditionally sanctioned controls on market behavior is not a cause of the dysfunctional status of the market among the Mossi, but a result of it. The need for such controls has not yet been strong enough to generate the necessary changes from within the context of Mossi traditional culture, and external controls based on European models have not been effective. The resultant anarchy in the Mossi marketplace is mild only because the market is of limited importance.

However, one of the results of political independence in Yatenga as part of the new Voltaic Republic appears to be a continued emphasis on increased participation in the market sector of the economy. If this increase in market participation is not paralleled by an increase in productivity among the Mossi farmers working on their own land, the market will make it possible, and in many instances, necessary, for the Mossi to borrow against and even to sell their land, to borrow against the value of their labor, and to

go into debt for food. When this occurs, their culture will be transformed, and another group of once autonomous African farmers
will be on the way to becoming landless or land-hungry proletarians.

This assertion is not made in opposition to the market as an
institution, but because it is cogent to an important contention:
Mossi technology, at its present level of development, makes
reliance on the exchange processes of redistribution and reciprocity
necessary for the equitable allocation of goods and work essential
to the maintenance of the material base of Mossi culture.

TECHNOLOGY AND SOCIAL ORGANIZATION

The integration between technology and Mossi social organization is just as close. Many aspects of this relationship have already
been identified within the discussion of Mossi economic organization. Obviously the economic system and the social organization
developed together. The distinction between them exists most
concretely in the mind's eye of the anthropologist. More certainly
there than in the perception of the Mossi who would argue with
good cause that the two institutions are inextricably linked. Which
of the two was more important in effecting the development of the
other through time is, of course, a moot question. In the present,
however, the relation is clear. It is the economic system as its
organization is limited by the technology that affects the other
aspects of Mossi society.

Every component unit in the complex Mossi kinship system
derives an important aspect of its reason for being from the nature
of the technology and the economic relationships that follow from
it. The role of the elementary family has been described as it
relates to using the land, to organizing work, and to organizing the
distribution of the products of work. The same interdependent
relationship was detailed for the other units in the family system—
the polygynous family, the extended family, and the patriclan. The
regulation of land use and of work is similarly central to the
structure and function of the lineage system.

The economic functions of Mossi associations were also fully
indicated—the sentiments of bond friendship as they are constantly
reinforced by technological and economic services mutually rendered, the role of age grades as they provide a valuable community-

wide basis for economic adjustment to the technology, and joking alliances between lineages and communities, as they serve in the same way.

The absence of social stratification in Mossi society is also to be understood as a result of the relative unproductivity of Mossi technology, and of the accompanying economic system which inhibits the private accumulation of whatever surpluses there are. And finally, the castelike status of the Mossi smiths is attributable to, and perpetuated by, their special role in Mossi technology.

The interrelationship between Mossi technology and the social system is thrown into even sharper perspective as innovations in technology begin to occur—mostly, so far—outside Yatenga. There has already been a reference to the development of plantations in the less densely populated forest regions of Ghana and the Ivory Coast, and the consequent need for a supply of cheap labor which has led to the migration of Mossi workers, especially during the dry season. This has begun to precipitate alterations in the traditional organization of the social system by changing the structure of the extended family and weakening the authority of elders in the kin group. As such external technological innovations continue their effect is likely to be cumulative.[2]

TECHNOLOGY AND THE POLITICAL SYSTEM

The interrelationship between the political system of the Mossi and their indigenous technology is also evident in a variety of ways. The causal linkage has been indicated between low productivity, the consequent technological, and economic semiautonomy of the local community and the absence of need, at least in times of peace, for the maintenance of a strongly centralized political system either within or between Mossi communities. For reasons that are essentially technological, each community can and does maintain itself materially; economic and social ties between communities are peripheral to the resolution of the problem of economic or social survival.

This assertion can be further validated by reference to the historical record.[3] Once many Mossi were warriors. The indigenous

2. See Hammond 1959, especially page 254 ff.
3. The documentary record is scant and diffuse, but see Balima 1959 ; Beauminy 1925 ; Chéron 1925 ; Durrieu 1934 ; and Kabore 1960.

system of land use was an important cause of the wars or raids they sometimes made. As farmlands at the frontiers of Mossi territory became impoverished from overcultivation and erosion, or inadequate as the consequence of population growth, warfare provided a means of acquiring needed additional land. Necessary reliance on aggression for territorial expansion strengthened the authority of the Mossi chiefs, who were leaders in war, and of their king, who was the most powerful war leader of all. Warfare provided a means of increasing the wealth of the chiefs and the kings, and also a means of rewarding, and thus retaining, their followers. This required more goods than the relatively unproductive technology of the Mossi could supply. Reliance on warfare and raiding as a means of increasing the supply of land and other goods both created the problem and provided the solution.

TECHNOLOGY AND RELIGION

Interconnections between the religious system of the Mossi and their technology are, in some ways, most readily perceptible of all the relationships that have been described. First consider ancestor worship. That aspect of the role of the ancestral spirits that is of greatest importance relates to their responsibility for seeing that the traditions of proper land use, which they established, are maintained. No crimes are more serious than misusing, defiling, or alienating the land which belongs to these spirits and to their descendants. Such crimes are punished by sickness or death. Thus this aspect of Mossi religion, which presumably developed with, and in response to, the technology, serves as a significant source of technological conservatism. Innovation is a violation of the ancestors' will. The question whether the resultant material benefits are worth the risk of supernatural punishment is always considered seriously, and often effectively inhibits technological change.

Those several manifestations of the Mossi deity which control the natural environment have a similarly close relationship to the technology of the Mossi. The very character of these beings, the powers with which they are endowed, represent a remarkably explicit projection of the farmers' concern with the problem of controlling those aspects of the natural environment that affect their livelihood. The aspect of the deity responsible for the rains, the

"So long as the traditional technology persists unmodified . . . life in the villages of Yatenga will go on as it always has, changing—but very slowly."

aspect of the deity that insures the fertility of the soil, the aspect of the deity that provides for vigorous plant growth—the characteristics of all these supernatural entities are clearly a consequence of the manner in which the Mossi are related by their technology to nature.

Again, as with the interrelationship between technology and the Mossi social system, the causal connection between technology and Mossi religion is made especially evident when technological innovation occurs. Some indication has been made of the manner in which the increased rate of conversion to Islam among the Mossi may be explained as a response to such innovation—most markedly among migrant laborers working away from Yatenga, either on the plantations of Ghana and the Ivory Coast or in cities in the Western Sudan itself. These young men are away from home for several months to several years. During this time they find themselves in milieux lacking the sources of supernatural support to which they are accustomed. Neither the places—the ritual areas and ancestral shrines—nor the persons—the Earth priests and lineage elders—nor the times—the religious rituals that mark the phases of the technological cycle—none of the traditional means by which the Mossi control their relations to the supernatural are present in these foreign regions.

But they are often among peoples who possess an alternative system for the regulation of relations with the supernatural: Islam. The Mossi migrants are quickly converted. This religious change affects not only their relationship to the supernatural but also to their fellow men. So long as they remain pagan in the eyes of the alien peoples among whom they work, they cannot anticipate social acceptance, economic cooperation or, what is most important, assistance if they should fall ill and ritual attention if they should die. Conversion to Islam solves this problem because it serves as a means of relating to non-Mossi by providing a basis for common identity. Brotherhood in Islam transcends historic, ethnic, and linguistic differences which otherwise set them apart.

When they return to their own communities and farms in Yatenga, the Mossi become once again dependent upon traditional sources of supernatural support. Usually they have by this time inherited positions of some status in their kin groups and are responsible for the maintenance of themselves and their growing elementary families by farming in the traditional way. When this occurs, it becomes necessary for them to reactivate their relationships with the ancestral spirits and the deities of nature. They do so with alacrity.

These indications of a causal relationship between the traditional technology of the Mossi and their religious system are also to be observed among Mossi settlers established on the newly developed lands of the Niger Irrigation Project[4] in Mali.

For other Mossi, who remain in Yatenga but abandon their roles in the traditional technology, by becoming merchants or petty members of the new political administration, the espousal of Islam serves equally well as a means of adjustment, by providing an ideological rationale for partial withdrawal from full participation in the network of redistributive and reciprocal ties that are functionally integrated with the traditional technology and supported by the indigenous religious system.

So far the relative continuity of traditional Mossi culture is to be explained by the absence of technological innovation in Yatenga. So long as the indigenous technology persists unmodified, there is no internal basis, or need, for economic change. So long as the technology and the economic system are not innovated, there is no need for change in the social system. So long as the economic and social systems remain unaltered, there is no occasion for change in the organization of the political system. And traditional Mossi religion, which serves to sanction the structure and the functional integration of each of these institutions is similarly perpetuated.

Life in the villages of Yatenga will go on as it always has, changing—but very slowly.

4. See Hammond, 1959, 1960, and 1963.

A SELECTED BIBLIOGRAPHY
OF THE MOSSI

GENERAL

1. Alexandre, O. *La Langue Mŏré,* Dakar: Institut Français d'Afrique Noire, 1953, 2 vols.
2. Balima, S. A. "Notes sur l'Organisation de l'Empire Mossi." Paris: *Mémoires de l'Institut des Hautes Études d'Outre-Mer,* n.d.
3. Binger, Louis. *Du Niger au Golfe de Guinée par le Pays Kong et le Moss.* Paris: Hatchette et Cie., 1892.
4. Carrier-Moulins. "Monographie du Cercle de Ouagadougou." Dakar: Senegal, *Archives Inédites du Haut-Senegal-Niger, Gouvernement Générale de l'Afrique Occidentale Francaise,* 1909.
5. Chaudron, M. "Les Races de le Volta Noire," *Revue des Troupes Coloniales,* 129 (March, 1913).
6. Delobsom, A. A. D. *L'Empire du Mogho-Naba, Coutumes des Mossi de la Haute-Volta.* Paris: Domat-Montchrestien, 1953.
7. Dupont, A. "La Rapide Evolution des Africains dans la Haute-Volta," *Marchés Coloniaux,* No. 163 (1948), No. 165, 1949.
8. Fau, M. "Monographie du Cercle de Ouahigouya," (typewritten). Ouahigouya, Voltaic Republic, *Archives Inédites du Cercle de Ouahigouya,* 1955.
9. Francois, von. "Voyage à Salaga et au Mossi," *Mitt. aus Deutschen Schutzgeb,* 1888, p. 143.

10. Franc, G. "Le Pays de Yatenga: Monographie du Cercle de Ouahigouya." Paris: *Mémoire de l'Institut des Hautes Études d'Outre-Mer,* n.d.
11. Hilton, T. E. "Mossi Country," *Universitas,* Vol. 4, 1 (December, 1959), pp. 7–8.
12. Hoffmann, Michel. *Problèmes D'Enseignement en Haute Volta, Monographie d'un Village Mossi.* Bordeaux: Institute des Sciences Humaines Appliquées de l'Université de Bordeaux, 1957.
13. Izard-Heritier, F., and M. Izard. *Les Mossi du Yatenga.* Bordeaux Institut des Sciences Humaines Appliquées de l'Université de Bordeaux, 1959.
14. Kiba, S. "Un Village de Haute-Volta," *Revue de l'Action Populaire,* Vol. 139 (Juin, 1960), pp. 757–66.
15. Kollman, E. "Among the Mossi," *White Fathers,* Vol. 94 (1956), pp. 7–9.
16. Lajus, Michel. "La Republique Voltaique," *Lq Revue Francaise,* (November, 1959).
17. Lambert, M. "Le Pays Mossi," *Bulletin de la Société de Geographie de l'Afrique Occidentale Française,* Vol. 30 (Juin, 1908).
18. Le Moal, G. "Le Peuple Mossi," *Encyclopedie Mensuelle d'Outre-Mer,* Vol. 3 (Février, 1954), pp. 17–21.
19. Mangin, E. "Les Mossi," *Anthropos,* Vol. 9, 1–2, (Janvier–Avril, 1914), pp. 98–124; 3–4 (Mai–Aout, 1914), pp. 477–93; 5–6 (Septembre–Décembre, 1914), pp. 705–36; 10–11, 1–2 (Janvier–Avril, 1915–1916), pp. 187–217; 3–4 (Mai Aout, 1915–1916), pp. 323–31.
20. Marc, A. "Note sur la Geographie du Mossi," *La Geographie,* Vol. 19 (1900), pp. 45–54.
21. ———. *Le Pays Mossi.* Paris: Larose, 1909.
22. Matthews, J. H. "English Mole Vocabulary," *Gold Coast Review* (January–June, 1929), pp. 73–95.
23. Noire, C. *Monographie du Cercle de Ouahigouya* (typewritten). Cercle de Ouahigouya, Upper Volta, 1904.
24. Pehuat, Yves, and Paul Roumba. "Vallée du Sourou Problèmes Humaines" (Rapport Preleminaire). Bordeaux: *Institut des Sciences Humaines Appliquées, Université de Bordeaux,* 1958.
25. Rattray, R. S. *An Elementary Mole Grammar, With A Vocabulary.* Oxford: Clarendon Press, 1918.
26. Tauxier, L. *Le Noir du Soudan, Pays Mossi et Gourounsi.* Paris: Larose, 1912.
27. ———. *Nouvelles Notes Sur Le Mossi et Le Gourounsi.* Paris: Larose, 1924.
28. ———. *Le Noir du Yatenga.* Paris: Larose, 1917.
29. Vadier, M. *Monographie du Cercle de Ouahigouya* (typewritten). Ouahigouya, Upper Volta, 1909.
30. Voulet, L. "Au Mossi et au Gourounsi," *Bulletin de la Société de Geographie,* 19 (1897), pp. 729–51.

HISTORY

1. Abatucci, S. "Les Médecins Explorateurs, La Mission du docteur Crozat au Mossi en 1890." Paris: *Société de Médecine Publique et de Génie Sanitaire, 1928.*

2. Borderier, P. "Avec les Mossis de la Haute Volta," *Tropiques,* N.S. 47 (Janvier, 1949), pp. 13–21.

3. Chéron, G. "Contribution à l'Histoire du Mossi. Traditions Relatives au Cercle de Naya (Haute-Volta)," *Bulletin du Comité d'Études Historiques et Scientifiques de l'Afrique Occidentale Française,* Vol. 7, 4 (Octobre–Décembre, 1924), pp. 635–91.

4. Crozat. "Rapport sur une Mission au Mossi (1890)," *Journal de la Republique Française,* Vols. 5–9 (Octobre, 1891).

5. Delobsom, Dim. *L'Empire du Mogho-Naba.* Paris: Domat-Montchrestien, 1933.

6. Es-Sadi, A. *Tarikh-es-Soudan.* Paris: Leroux, 1900.

7. Gill, J. W. *The Moshi Tribe: A Short History.* Accra, Ghana, 1924.

8. Houis, M. "Mouvements Historiques et Communautés Linguistiques dans l'Ouest Africain," *L'Homme,* Vol. 1, 3 (Septembre–Décembre, 1961), pp. 72–91.

9. Mauny, R. "État Actuel de nos Connaissances sur la Prehistoire et l'Archeologie de la Haute-Volta," *Notes Africaines,* Vol. 73 (Janvier, 1957), pp. 16–25.

10. Noll, N. "Le Mossi, La Mission de Lt. Voulet," *La Tour du Monde,* XXXII (Aout 14, 1897), p. 257.

11. Pageard, R. "Réflexions sur l'Histoire des Mossi," *L'Homme,* Vol. 2, 1 (Janvier–Avril, 1962), pp. 111–15.

12. Prost, A. "Notes Sur l'Origine des Mossi," *Bulletin de l'Institut Francais Afrique Noire,* Vol. 15, 3 (Juillet, 1953), pp. 1933–38.

13. Randau, R. "Au Pays des Mossi," *Bulletin de la Société de Geographie d'Álger et d'Afrique du Nord,* Vol. 39 (1934), p. 427.

14. Rouamba, Tensoré. "Mission d'Énquete en Haute-Volta," *Cahiers d'Études Africaines,* No. 10, 1962, pp. 299–301.

15. Savonnet, G. "Notes sur Quelques Ruines de la Region de Léo (Haute Volta)," *Notes Africaines,* 71 (Juillet, 1956), pp. 65–7.

16. Skinner, Elliott P. "The Mossi and Traditional Sudanese History," *The Journal of Negro History,* Vol. 43, 2 (April, 1958), pp. 121–31.

17. Voulet. *Mission au Mossi et au Gourounsi (1896–1897).* Paris: Chapelot, 1898.

18. Vuillet, J. "Essai d'Interprétation de Traditions Légendaires sur les Origines des Vieux Empires Soudanais," *Chroniques Mensuelles des Seánces de l'Academie des Sciences Coloniales,* Vol. 10 1950), pp. 268–88.

19. Zahan, D. "Pour Une Histoire des Mossi du Yatenga," *L'Homme,* Vol. 1, 2 (Mai–Août, 1961), pp. 5–22.

YATENGA

TECHNOLOGY

1. "L'Alimentation des Mossi de la Region de Ouahigouya," *Bulletin d'Information de l'Afrique Occidentale Française*, Vol. 136 (Octobre 15, 1952), pp. 5–8.
2. Dupont. "Rapport sur une Mission de Vaccine Effectuée dans le Cercle de Ouahigouya de Juin 1909 à Janvier 1910," *Journal de l'Afrique Occidentale Française* (1911), p. 69.
3. Gentil, P. "Le Forgeron Mossi." Dakar, Sénégal: *Archives Inédites de l'Institut Français d'Afrique Noire*, 1937.
4. Heuzey, J. A. *Rapport sur l'Artisanat Indiqène: Baoule, Lobi, Mossi, Bobo*. Dakar: Sénégal: *Archives Inédites de l'Institut Français d'Afrique Noire*, 1963.
5. Holas, B. "Teinturiers Mossi à Dimbokro (Côte d'Ivoire)," *Notes Africaines*, Vol. 38 (Avril, 1948), pp. 18–21.
6. Izard-Héritier, Françoise, and Michel Izard. *Aspects Humaines de l'Aménagement Hydro-Agricole de La Vallée Du Sourou*. Bordeaux: Institute des Sciences Humaines Appliquées de l'Université de Bordeaux, 1958, pp. 25–38, 44–65.
7. Kerharo, J. "Le Wilinwiga des Mossi *(guiera senegalensis Lam.)* ses Usages Therapeutiques Indigènes et son Application au Traitement des Diarrhées, Cholériformes," *Acta Tropica*, Vol. 5, 4 (1948), pp. 345–8.
8. Ouedraogo, J. and A. Prost. "Alimentation en Pays Mossi," *Première Conference des Africanistes de l'Ouest*. Dakar, Sénégal: Institut Français d'Afrique Noire, 1951, Vol. 2, p. 567.
9. Prost, A. "Les Aliments Crus Chez l'Indigène Mossi-Boussance," *Notes Africaines*, 11 (Juillet–Octobre, 1941), pp. 55–6.
10. Savvonet, G. "Methodes Employées par Certaines Populations de Haute-Volta pour Lutter Contre l'Erosion," *Notes Africaines*, Vol. 78 (Avril, 1958), pp. 38–40.
11. Serre, A. *Aspects Alimentaires et Nutritionnels de la Haute-Volta Est, (Bobo-Dioulasso)*. Paris: ORANA, 1953, p. 94.
12. ———. *Aspects Qualitatifs de l'Alimentation Mossi. Aliments et Mode de Préparation, (Bobo-Dioulasso)*. Paris: ORANA, 1953, p. 81.
13. Tricart, J. "Deux Types de Production Agricole aux Environs d'Odienne (Haute Cote d'Ivoire)," *Bulletin de l'Institut Français d'Afrique Noire*, Vol. 19, 1–2 (Janvier–Avril, 1957), pp. 284–94.
14. Zahan, D. "L'Habitation Mossi," *Bulletin de l'Institut Français d'Afrique Noire*, Vol. 12 (Janvier, 1950), pp. 223–91.

ECONOMIC ORGANIZATION

1. Balima, S. A. "Notes on the Social and Labor Situation in the

Republic of the Upper Volta," *International Labor Review*, Vol. 4 (October, 1960), pp. 358–62.

2. Hammond, Peter B. "The Niger Project: Some Cultural Sources of Conflict," in W. H. Lewis (ed.), *Emerging Africa*, Washington, D.C.: Public Affairs Press, 1963, pp. 12–28.

3. ———. "Economic Change and Mossi Acculturation," in W. R. Bascom and M. J. Herskovits (eds.), *Continuity and Change in African Cultures*, Chicago: Chicago University Press, 1959, pp. 238–56.

4. ———. "Management in Economic Transition," in W. E. Moore and A. S. Feldman (eds.), *Labor Commitment and Social Change in Developing Areas*, New York: Social Science Research Council, 1960, pp. 109–22.

5. Le Moal, G. "Un Aspect de L'Émigration: La Fixation des Voltaïques au Ghana," *Bulletin de l'Institut Français d'Afrique Noire*, Vol. 22, 3–4 (1960), pp. 446–54.

6. Ouedraogo, J., and A. Prost. "La Propriété Foncière chez les Mossi," *Notes Africaines*, Vol. 38 (Avril, 1948), pp. 16–18.

7. Rouch, J. "Migrations au Ghana," *Journal de la Société des Africanistes*, Vol. 76, 1–2 (1956), pp. 33–126.

8. Skinner, Elliott P. "Labour Migration and its Relationship to Sociocultural Change in Mossi Society," *Africa*, Vol. 30, 4 (October, 1960), pp. 375–401.

9. ———. "Trade and Markets Among the Mossi People," in P. Bohannan and G. Dalton (eds.), *Markets in Africa*, Evanston, Ill.: Northwestern University Press, 1962.

10. Zahan, D. "Notes sur les Marches Mossi du Yatenga," *Africa*, Vol. 24, 4 (October, 1954), pp. 370–7.

SOCIAL ORGANIZATION

1. Bernard, Jean. "Structures et Relations Sociales Bisa," *Cahiers d'Études Africaines*, Vol. 18, v.5(2) (1965).

2. Dubourg, J. "La vie des Paysans Mossi. Le Village de Taghalla," *Les Cahiers d'Outre-Mer*, Vol. 40 (Octobre–Décembre, 1957), pp. 285–324.

3. Hammond, Peter B. "The Functions of Indirection in Communication," in J. D. Thompson *et al.* (eds.), *Comparative Studies in Administration*, Pittsburgh: University of Pittsburgh Press, 1959, pp. 183–94.

4. Laffitte, N. "La Hiérarcharchie Mossi," *Bulletin d'Informations et de Renseignments*, Vol. 193 (Août, 1938), pp. 159–65.

5. Marie-André du Sacré-Coeur (Soeur). "La Femme Mossi, sa Situation Juridique," *L'Ethnographie*, Vols. 33–34 (1937), pp. 101–5, 35–36 (1938), pp. 15–33.

6. ———. "La Condition de la Femme au Mossi," *Grands Lacs,* Vol. 54 (1937–1938), pp. 177–81.

7. Ouedrago, J. "La Polygamie en Pays Mossi," *Notes Africaines,* Vol. 50 (Avril, 1951), pp. 46–52.

8. Skinner, Elliott P. "The Mossi Pogsioure," *Man,* Vol. 60 (February, 1960), pp. 20–3.

9. ———. "Intergenerational Conflict Among the Mossi: Father and Son," *The Journal of Conflict Resolution,* Vol. 5, 1 (March, 1961), pp. 55–60.

10. ———. "The Effect of Co-Residence of Sister's Sons on African Corporate Patrilineal Descent Groups," *Cahiers d'Études Africaines,* Vol. 4 (1964), pp. 464–78.

POLITICAL ORGANIZATION

1. Balima, S. A. *Notes sur l'Organisation de l'Empire Mossi.* Paris: Mémoires de l'Institut des Hautes Etudes d'Outre-Mer, n.d.

2. Beauminy, A. de. "Une Féodalité en Afrique Occidentale Française: les Etats Mossi," *Renseignments Coloniaux et Documents,* Vol. 35, 1 (Janvier, 1925), pp. 24–36.

3. Chéron, G. "La Cour de Bousouma Naba," *Bulletin du Comité d'Etudes Historiques et Scientifiques de l'Afrique Occidentale Francaise,* Vol. 8, 2 (Avril–Juin, 1925), pp. 304–12.

4. ———. "L'Art Militaire Mossi," *Bulletin du Comité d'Etudes Historiques et Scientifiques de l'Afrique Occidentale Francaise,* Vol. 3, 3 (Juillet–Septembre, 1925), pp. 509–12.

5. Delobsom Dim. "Le Mogho Naba et sa Cour," *Bulletin du Comité d'Etudes Historiques et Scientifiques de l'Afrique Occidentale Francaise,* Vol. 11, 3 (Juillet–Septembre, 1928), pp. 386–421.

6. Kaboré, Tomkoudougou. "Caractère 'Feodal' du Système Politique Mossi," *Cahiers d'Études Africaines,* No. 8, 1961, pp. 609–23.

7. Prost, A. "L'Empire Mossi," *Grands Lacs,* Vol. 54 (1937–1938), pp. 145–9.

8. Skinner, Elliott. "An Analysis of the Political Organization of the Mossi People," *Transactions of the New York Academy of Sciences,* Vol. II, 19, 8 (June, 1957), pp. 740–50.

9. ———. "Traditional and Modern Patterns of Succession to Political Office Among the Mossi of the Voltaic Republic," *Journal of Human Relations,* Vol. 8, 3/4 (1960), pp. 394–406.

10. ———. *The Mossi of Upper Volta.* Stanford, Stanford University Press, 1964.

11. Verger, P. "Le Yatenga Naba de Ouahigouya," *Revue de Voyages* (Janvier, 1939), p. 23.

RELIGION

1. Arnould, Charles. "Les Fêtes au Yatenga (Cercle de Ouahigouya)," *Notes Africaines,* Vol. 42 (Avril, 1949), pp. 38–45.
2. Benquey. "Considerations sur l'Islam Africain (Haute Cote d'Ivoire)," *Bulletin du Comité d'Études Historiques et Scientifiques de l'Afrique Occidentale Francaise* (1921), pp. 678–88.
3. Delobsom Dim. "Les Procédés Divinatoires des Bagba (devins) au Mossi," *Journal of the Royal Anthropological Institute,* Vol. 43 (1933), pp. 182–212.
4. Derialle, G. I. "Superstitions en Pays Mossi," *Revue des Traditions Populaires,* Vol. 7 (1892), pp. 181–2.
5. Dittmer, K. "The Methods of Divination in the Upper Volta Region and Its Relation to the Hunter Culture," *Baessler-Archiv,* Vol. 1 (1958), pp. 1–60.
6. Granier, J. M. *Explication des Croyances Mossi: L'Homme-Neda.* Ouagadougou, Upper Volta, n.d.
7. Kaboré, D. Y. "Les Mangeuses d'Âmes Chez les Mossi," *Notes Africaines,* Vol. 24 (Octobre, 1944), pp. 17–18.
8. Laurent. "L'Initiation d'un Nouveau Féticheur en Haute-Volta," *Tropiques,* Vol. 53, 378 (Novembre, 1955), pp. 30–37.
9. "L'Ordalie Chez les Mossi," *Bulletin d'Information et de Renseignments,* Vol. 203 (1938), pp. 409–10.
10. Mandrin, J. "Le Signe du Croix Chez les Mossi," *Missions Catholiques* (Décembre, 1942), p. 182.
11. Ouédraogo, J. "Les Funérailles en Pays Mossi," *Bulletin de l'Institut Français d'Afrique Noire,* Series B, Vol. 12, 2 (Avril, 1950), pp. 441–55.
12. Skinner, Elliott P. "Christianity and Islam Among the Mossi," *American Anthropologist,* Vol. 60, No. 6 (December, 1958), pp. 1102–19.
13. ———. "The Diffusion of Islam in an African Society," *Annals of the New York Academy of Sciences,* Vol. 96, part 2 (January, 1962), pp. 659–69.
14. Vernau, M. "Curieuses Croyances des Nègres de la Haute-Volta Relatives aux Haches en Pierre Polie," *L'Anthropologie,* Vol. 33 (1923), pp. 294–5.

INDEX

INDEX

227